# Phonics Wonder

**LEVEL 3**

## Long Vowels

# Contents

# Lesson Plans of Phonics Wonder

### Letters & Sounds
New target combinations of sounds and related words are introduced with pictures.

### Read
Children practice reading words with the target sounds.

### Listen & Write
Children practice identifying and writing the target sounds.

### Listen & Read
Children practice listening and reading the target words.

### Read
Children practice reading sentences with the target words.

### Read Along!
Children further practice the target words reading simple story.

### Write Words
Children confirm their understanding of the target sounds and words by writing them.

## Key Features

The Review provides practice of the materials from the previous two units by using a variety of exercises for the target sounds of letters and words.

The Final Review reinforces the material with a variety of exercises such as the reading of brief stories that include the sight words and playing games.

The Final Test consists of 20 listening comprehension questions and 14 reading questions that cover the target sounds of letters and words.

# Introduction of the Multi-ROM

## Main Menu

 **Sound**

Children practice the target sounds and the corresponding words.

 **Words**

Children listen and repeat the words with the target sounds.

 **Chant**

Children listen and repeat the target sounds and words in the chant.

 **Read Along**

Children read and repeat the key words with the target letters in the sentences.

 **Game**

Children play games using the target letters and words.

 **Check-Up**

Children take a brief test by listening and reading the target letters and words.

## Details

Children listen and repeat the target sounds and words by watching the shape of a native speaker's mouth.

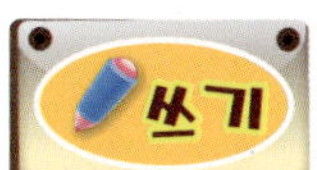


In **Words** corner, children write the target words by clicking their mouses.

Children record their own pronunciation of the target words and check it by comparing it to the recording of a native speaker's pronunciation.

# Unit 1 — Long Vowel a

Listen and repeat.  Track 01

   →    →    

a k e → c a k e → c a k e

 Track 02

**-ake**

c ake **cake**

l ake **lake**

b ake **bake**

r ake **rake**

Listen and repeat.  Track 03

a p e → c a p e → **c a p e**

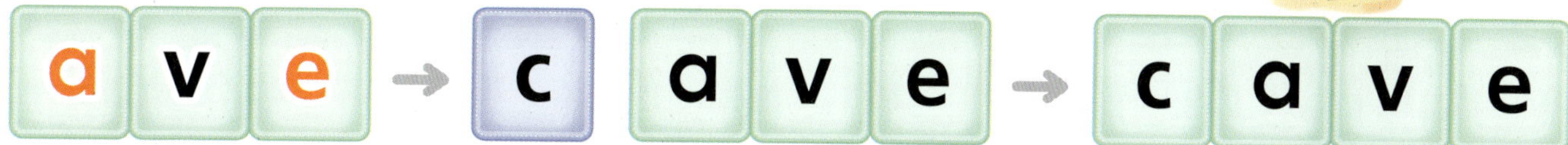

a v e → c a v e → **c a v e**

 Track 04

## -ape

c **ape** **cape**

t **ape** **tape**

## -ave

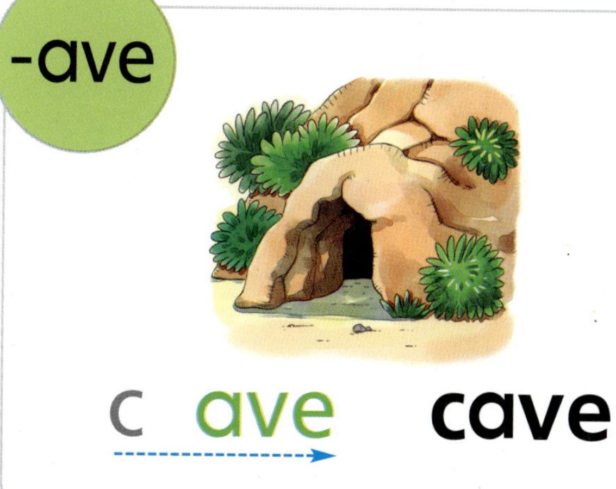

c **ave** **cave**

w **ave** **wave**

**Let's chant!** Track 05

# Read the word and circle the correct picture.

**1** lake

**2** cape

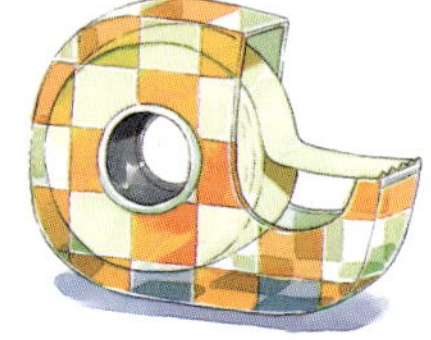  

**3** rake

**4** wave

**5** cake

**6** tape

Track 06

Listen to the word and circle the correct picture. 

Listen and circle the word. Then write it. 

**1** l h b a k e n

______________

**2** c a p e s g v

______________

**3** s b p c a k e

______________

**4** b w a v e c t

______________

# Write the correct word.

**1** 

A boy swims in the ___________ with
his dog.

| lake | rake |

**2** 

The fruit ___________ looks delicious.

| cave | cake |

**3** 

The man ___________s at the children.

| wave | bake |

**4**

The girl wears a red ___________ with
a hood.

| rake | cape |

**5** 

The man cleans the garden with a
___________.

| tape | rake |

Read Along!
Track 09

Kate and Jake play at the lake.
Kate gets some sand with a rake.
Jake gets some water from the lake.
They make a sand cake.

Oh, it's late. It's time to go.
Kate's mom waves at Kate.
Jake's mom waves at Jake.

**Trace and write the words.**

**-ake**

cake

lake

bake

rake

**-ape**

cape

tape

**-ave**

cave

wave

# Long Vowel a

Listen and repeat.  Track 10

a m e → n a m e → n a m e

a n e → c a n e → c a n e

Track 11

## -ame

n ame — **name**

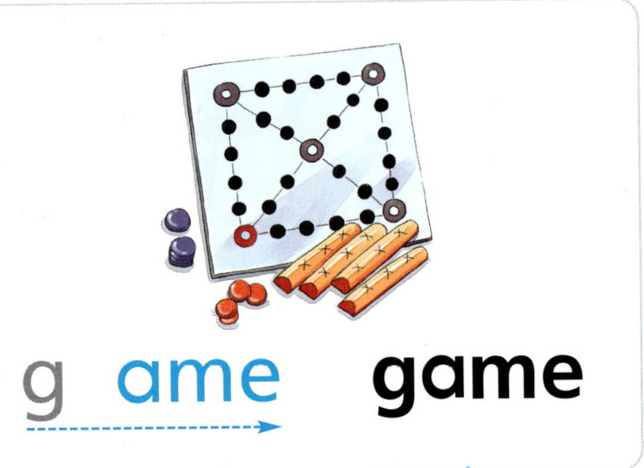

g ame — **game**

## -ane

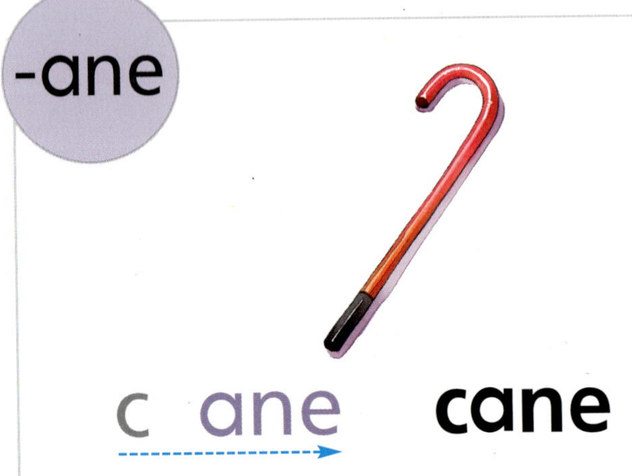

c ane — **cane**

l ane — **lane**

a g e → c a g e → c a g e

a s e → b a s e → b a s e

**-age**

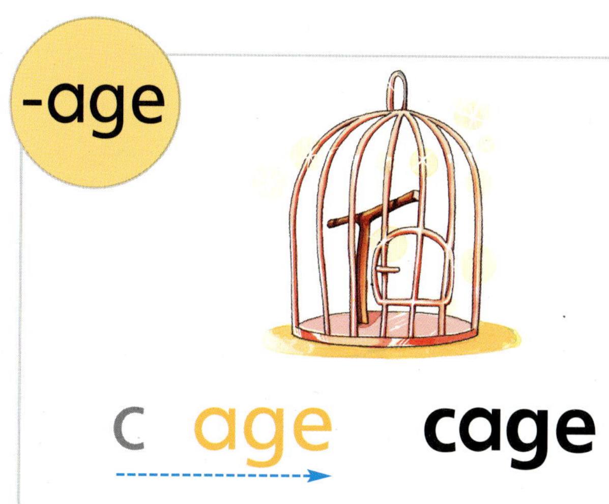

c age → cage

p age → page

**-ase**

b ase → base

v ase → vase

Read the word and circle the correct picture.

**1** cane

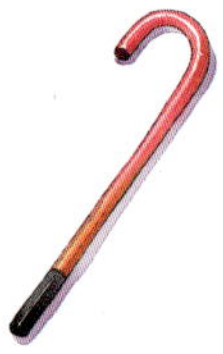

**2** vase

**3** name

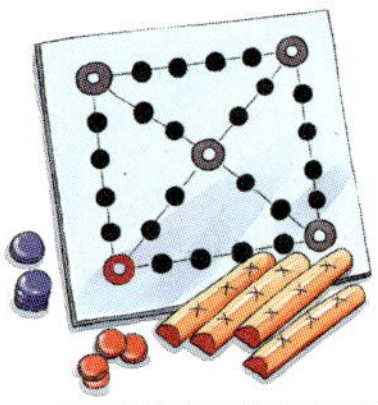

**4** lane

**5** page

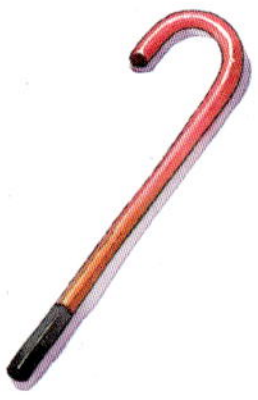

**6** game

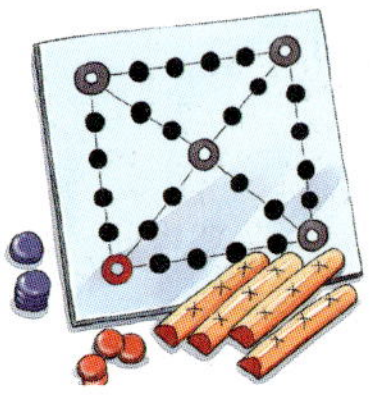

Track
15

**1**

ame    age

c

**2**

ane    ase

l

**3**

ame    ane

n

**4**

ase    age

b

**5**

age    ame

p

**6**

ane    ase

v

Listen to the word and circle the correct picture.  Track 16

Listen and circle the word. Then write it. Track 17

**1** 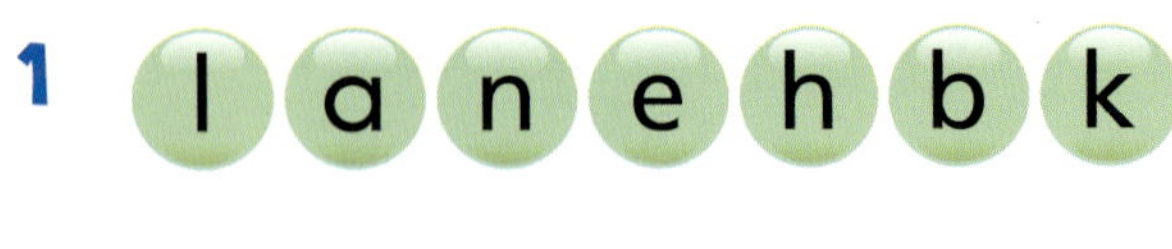

**2** w p c v a s e

**3** s n a m e k c

**4** v w p a g e t

Write the correct word.

**1**

A bird in the __________ sings.

cage | cane

**2**

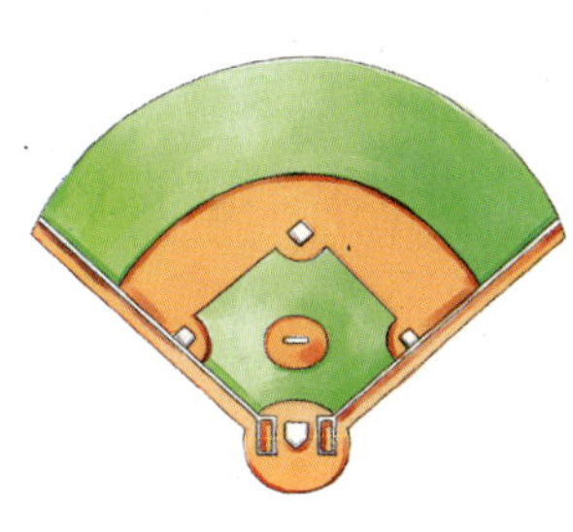

A baseball field has four __________s.

game | base

**3**

Look at __________ 27.

vase | page

**4**

Let's play a bingo __________.

game | lane

**5**

The dog's __________ is Coco.

base | name

# Read Along!



I name my dog Flame.

We love to play games together.

Flame, bring me a cane.

Oops! He brings a cage, not a cane.

Flame, bring me a vase.

Oops! He brings a vane, not a vase.

He is a very funny dog.

Trace and write the words.

**-ame**

name

game

**-ane**

cane

lane

**-age**

cage

page

**-ase**

base

vase

# Review 1

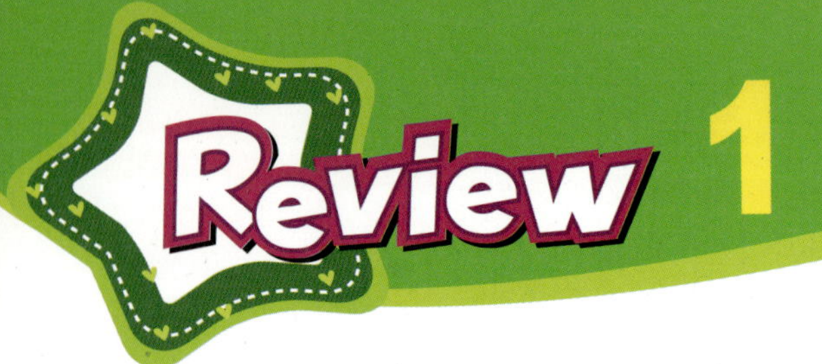

Match the correct letters to complete the word.

**1**

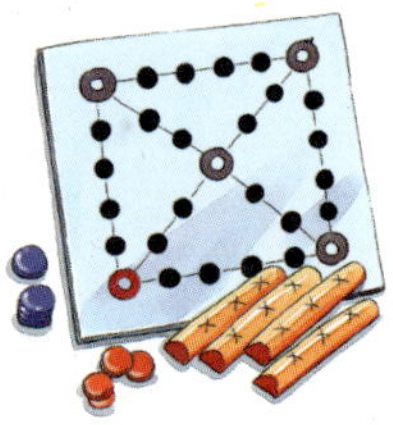

g •    • a m e    • a g e

**2**

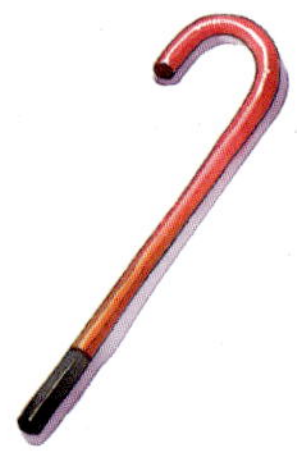

c •    • a v e    • a n e

**3**

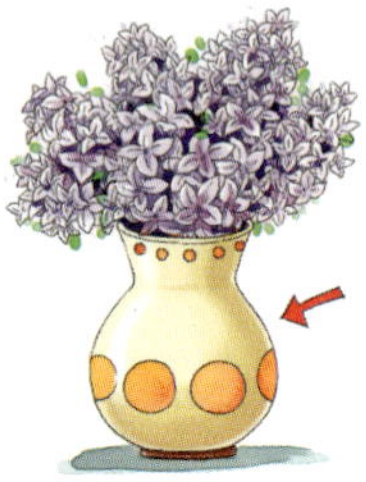

v •    • a n e    • a s e

**4**

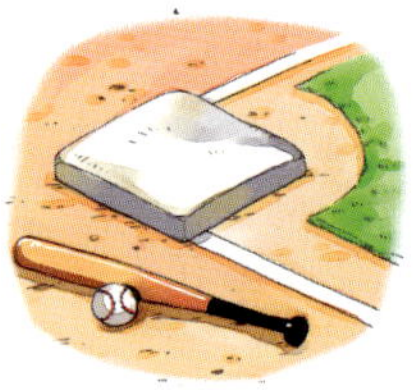

b •    • a s e    • a g e

**5**

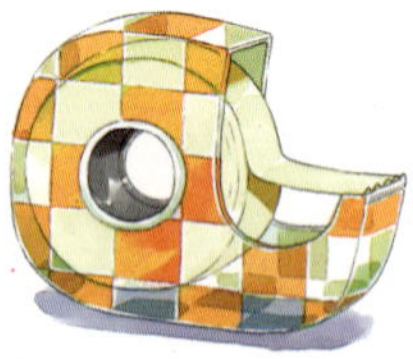

t •    • a p e    • a k e

**6**

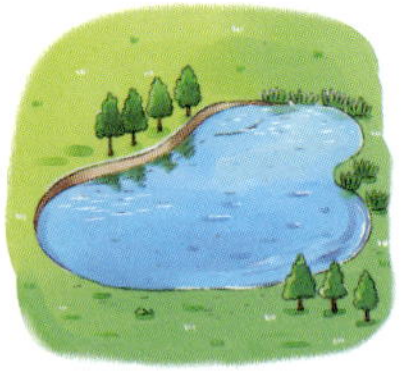

l •    • a v e    • a k e

**7**

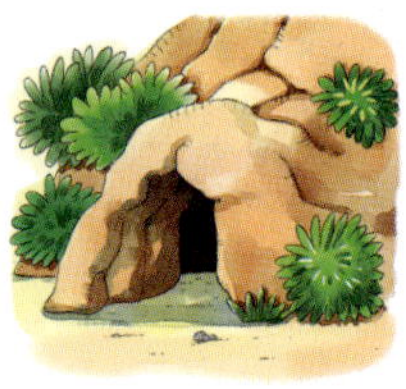

c •    • a v e    • a n e

**8**

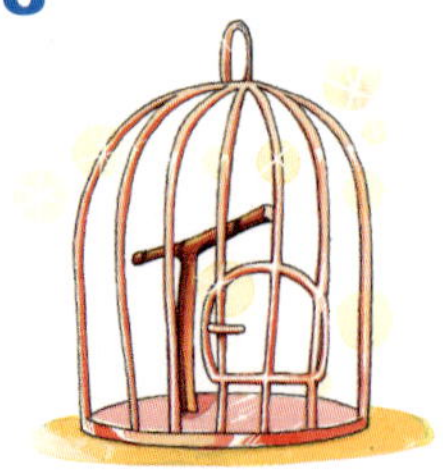

c •    • a p e    • a g e

# Listen to the word and circle the correct picture.  Track 19

**1**

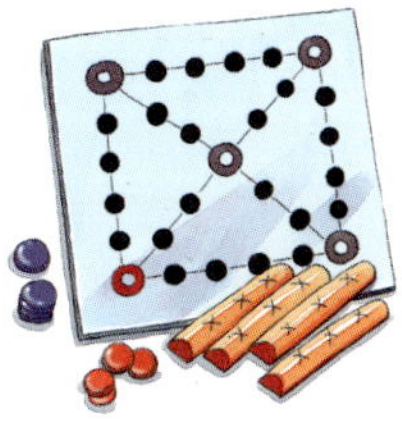

**2**

**3**

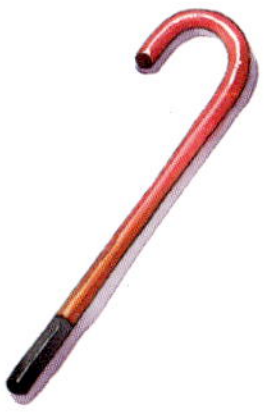

**4**

**5**

**6**

**7**

**8**

Listen and complete the word. Then match it to the correct picture. **Track 20**

1 c_____

2 b_____

3 c_____

4 c_____

5 l_____

6 l_____

7 b_____

8 v_____

9 p_____

10 w_____

11 g_____

12 c_____

# Listen and connect the correct words. Track 21

# Unit 3 · Long Vowel i

Listen and repeat. Track 22

i k e → b i k e → b i k e

i m e → d i m e → d i m e

Track 23

**-ike**

b ike  **bike**

h ike  **hike**

**-ime**

d ime  **dime**

t ime  **time**

  Track 24

  →     →  

i n e → p i n e → p i n e

  →     →  

i t e → k i t e → k i t e

Track 25

**-ine**

p ine   **pine**

l ine   **line**

**-ite**

k ite   **kite**

b ite   **bite**

  **Let's chant!** Track 26

Circle the picture ending with the given letters.

**1** -ine

**2** -ime

**3** -ite

**4** -ike

**5** -ite

**6** -ime

Listen to the word and circle the correct picture. Then complete the word. 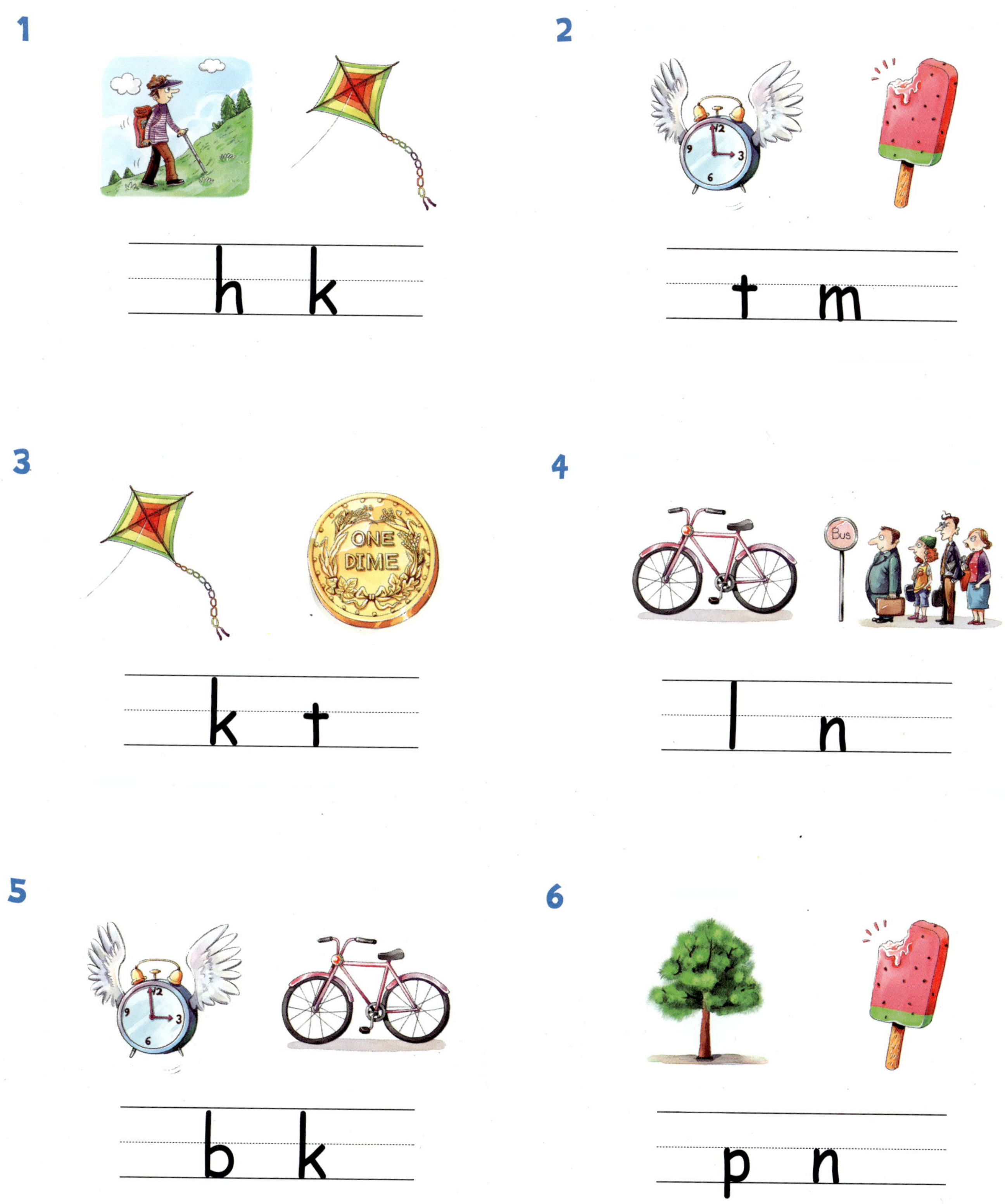

1

   h  k

2

   t  m

3

   k  t

4

   l  n

5

   b  k

6

   p  n

## Listen to the word and circle the correct picture. 

## Listen and unscramble the letters. Then write it. 

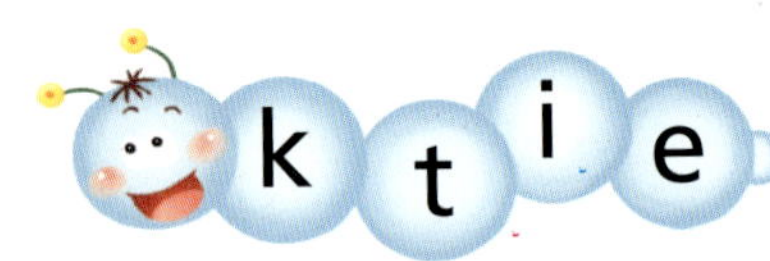

**1** i k e b

_______________________

**2** k t i e

_______________________

**3** i m t e

_______________________

**4** i n e p

_______________________

Write the correct letters in the blank. Then choose the correct picture.

**1** He rides a mountain b_ike____. b

-ite   -ike

**2** A d_________ is on the floor. ☐

-ike   -ime

**3** Kate flies a k_________ with her brother. ☐

-ite   -ine

**4** There is a p_________ by the house. ☐

-ine   -ime

**5** Ants go marching in a l_________. ☐

-ike   -ine

a

b

c

d

e

# Read Along!



"Oh, it's very sunny.

Let's bike to the pine."

"Okay, let's go outside."

"Oh, I'm very hungry.

Let's grab a bite."

"No, no, we have no dime."

"Oh, I'm very tired.

Let's take a break."

"Okay, we have some time."

Trace and write the words.

**-ike**

bike

hike

**-ime**

dime

time

**-ine**

pine

line

**-ite**

kite

bite

# Long Vowel i

Listen and repeat.  Track 31

i d e → r i d e → r i d e

i p e → p i p e → p i p e

 Track 32

**-ide**

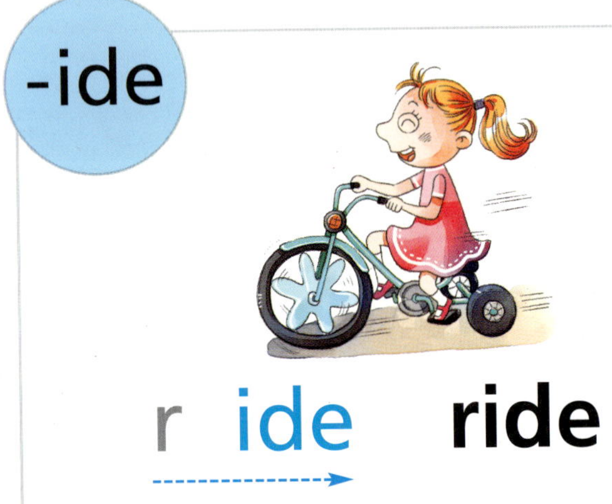

r ide  **ride**

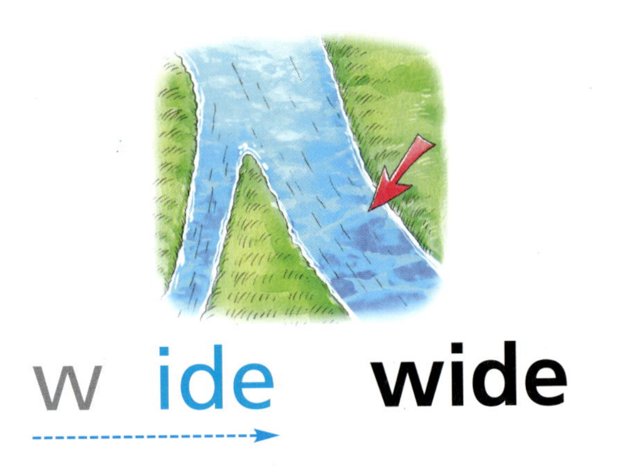

w ide  **wide**

**-ipe**

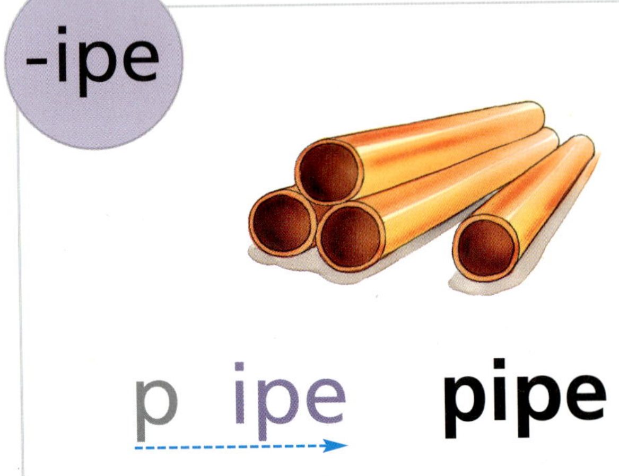

p ipe  **pipe**

w ipe  **wipe**

i r e → f i r e → f i r e

i v e → f i v e → f i v e

Track 34

**-ire**

f ire **fire**

t ire **tire**

**-ive**

f ive **five**

d ive **dive**

Let's chant! Track 35

35

# Circle the picture ending with the given letters.

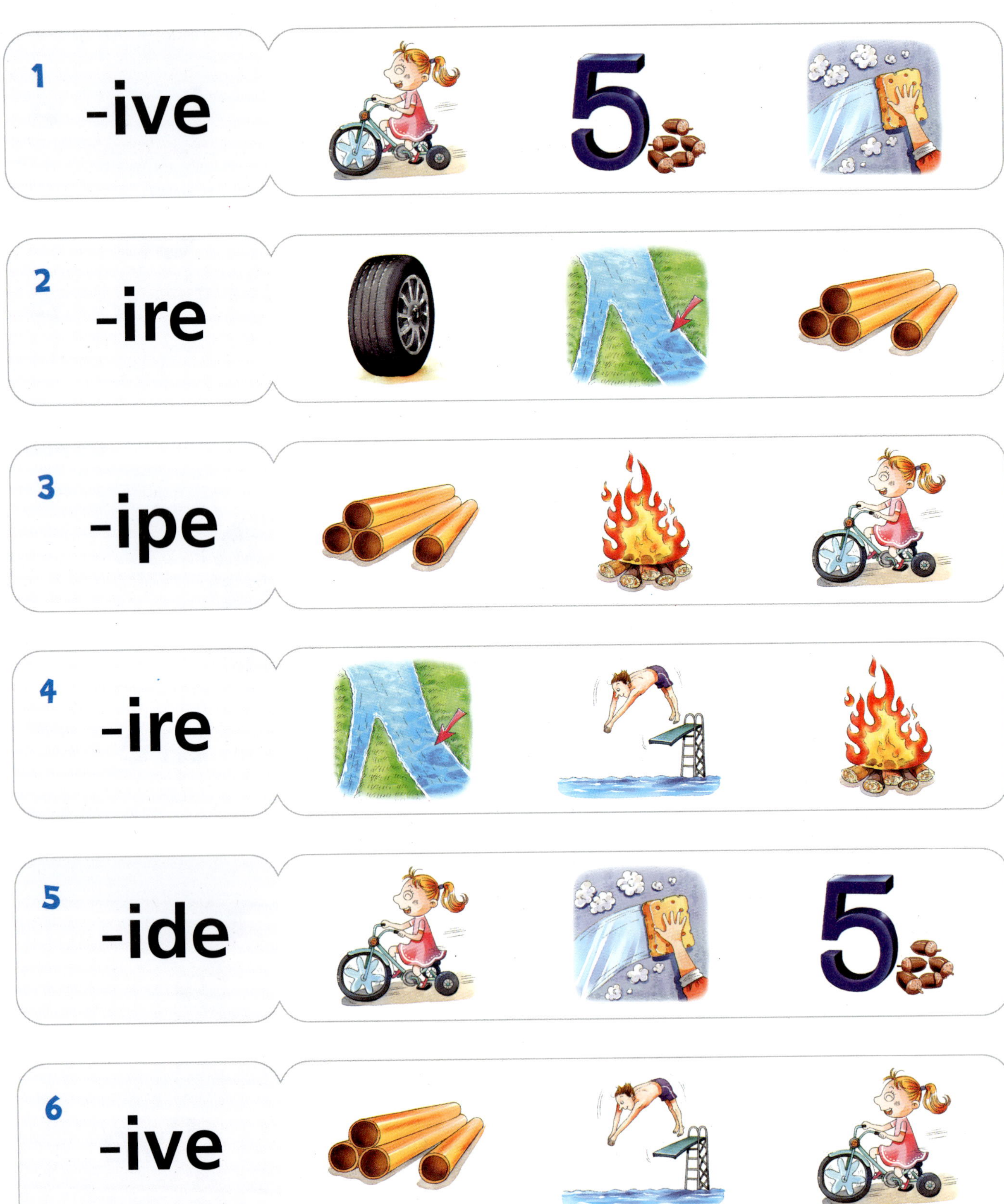

# Listen to the word and choose the correct letters. Then write it.

Track 36

**1**

ide    ipe

______________

w

**2**

ive    ire

______________

f

**3**

ire    ipe

______________

p

**4**

ive    ide

______________

f

**5**

ipe    ive

______________

w

**6**

ire    ipe

______________

t

Listen to the word and circle the correct picture. 

Listen and unscramble the letters. Then write it. 

**1**
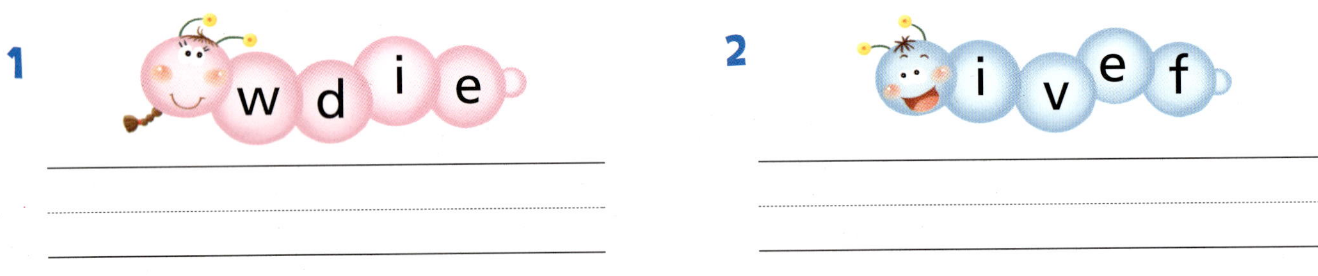


**2**


**3**
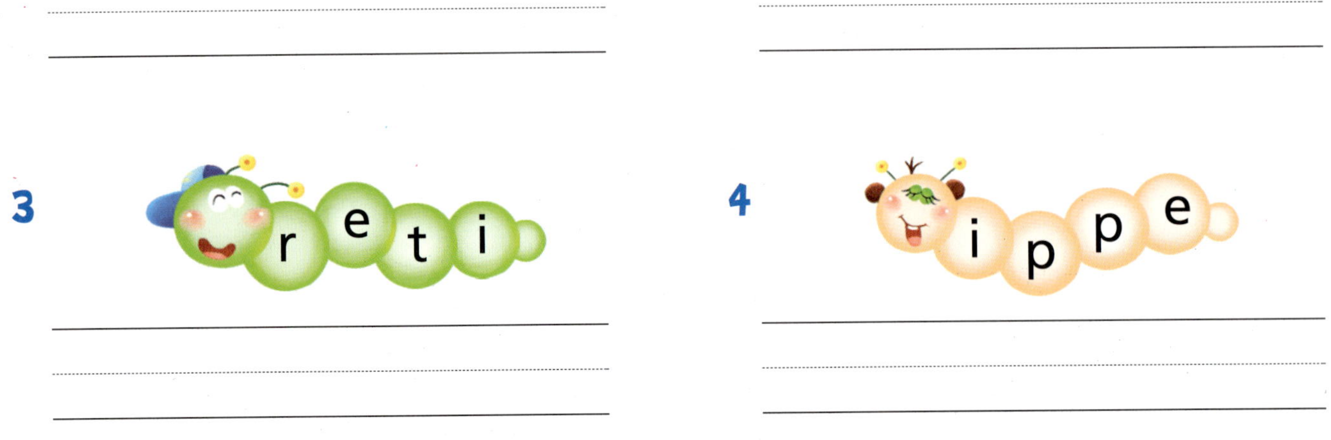


**4**

Write the correct letters in the blank. Then choose the correct picture.

**1** Water is pouring out the p___________. ☐

-ipe   -ide

**2** The school bus t___________ is flat. ☐

-ive   -ire

**3** The boys d___________ into the river. ☐

-ive   -ipe

**4** The girl w___________s her eyeglasses. ☐

-ipe   -ide

**5** F___________ little monkeys jump on the mat. ☐

-ire   -ive

a

b

c
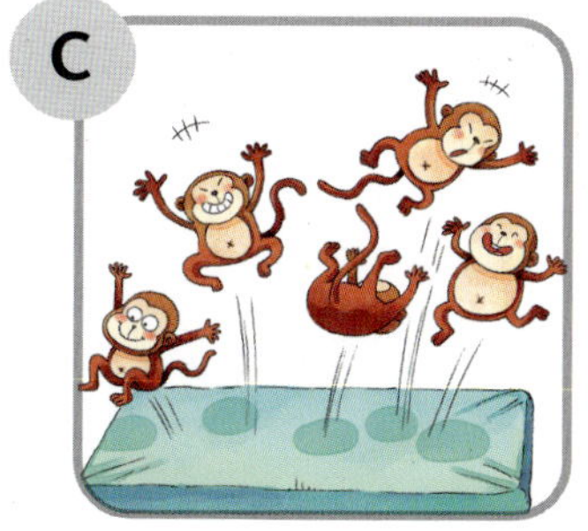

d

e

Five little pigs ride in a car.

They get to a wide river.

Five little pigs make a boat.

They get on the tire boat.

Oops, the water comes in.

Five little pigs dive into the river.

Trace and write the words.

**-ide**

ride

wide

**-ipe**

pipe

wipe

**-ire**

fire

tire

**-ive**

five

dive

## Match the correct letters to complete the word.

1

k
· i t e
· i p e

2

r
· i d e
· i v e

3

f
· i m e
· i v e

4

p
· i r e
· i n e

5

h
· i n e
· i k e

6

t
· i k e
· i m e

7

f
· i t e
· i r e

8

w
· i d e
· i p e

Listen to the word and circle the correct picture. Track 40

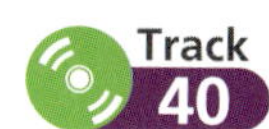

1

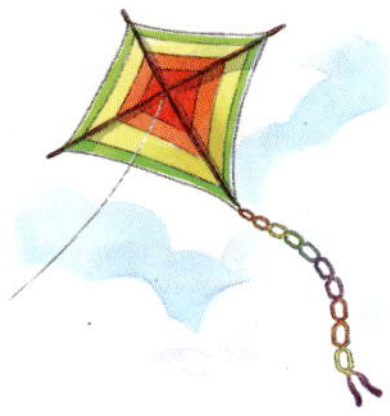
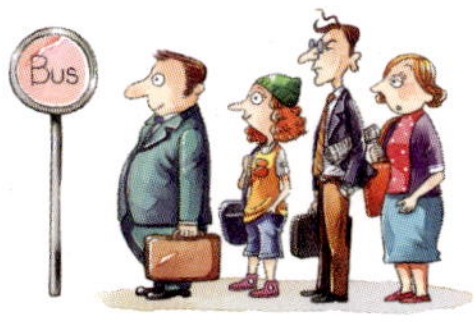


2

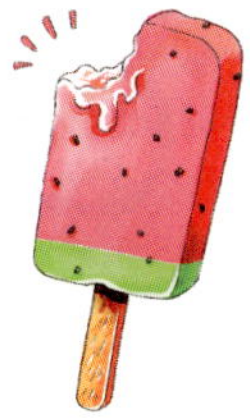
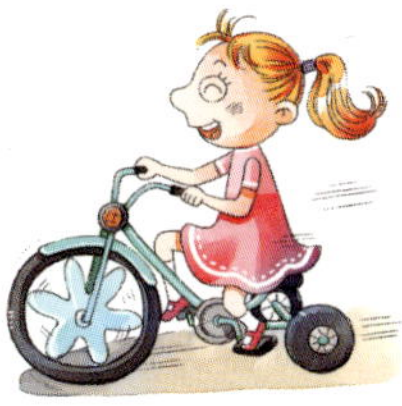

3

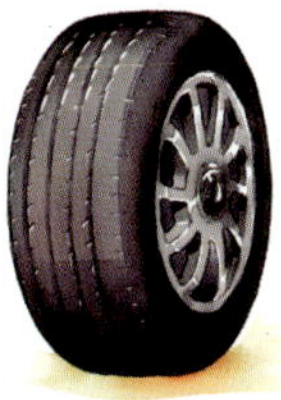
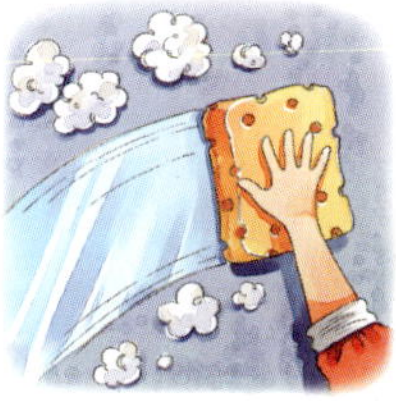

4

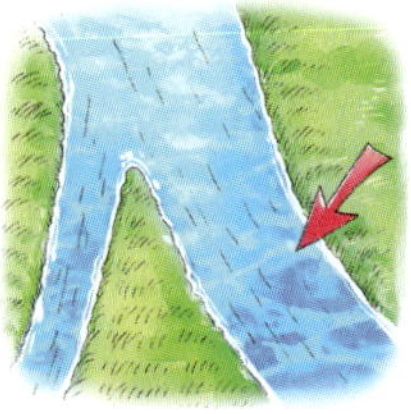
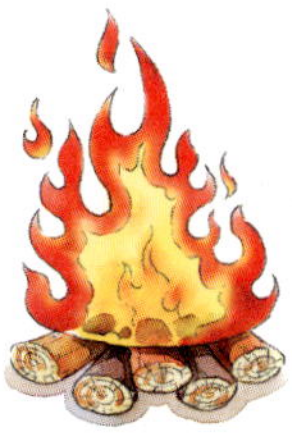

5

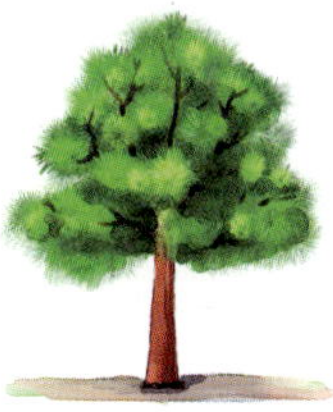
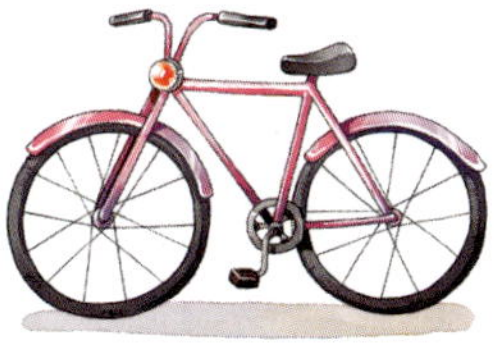

6

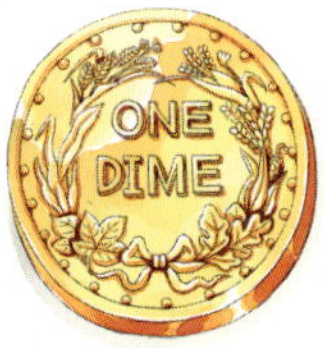

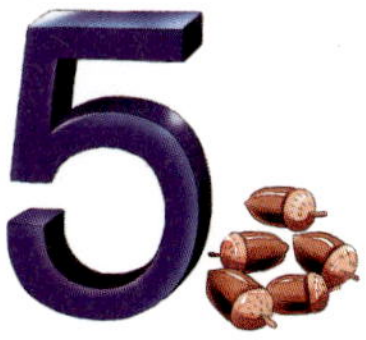

7

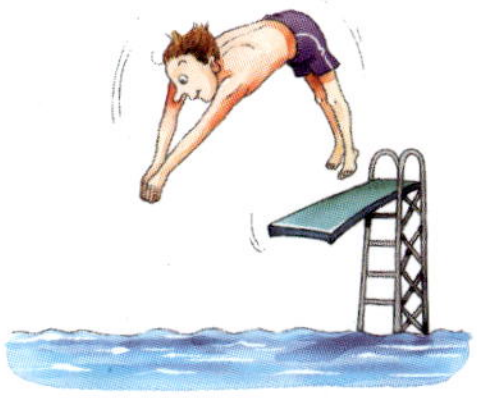
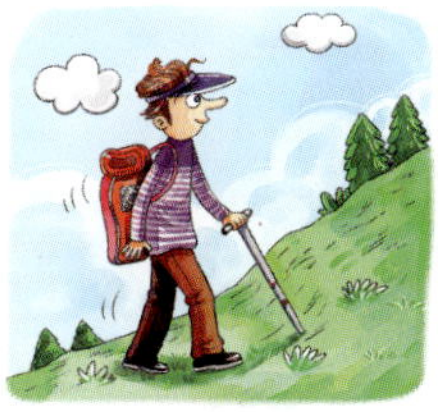

8

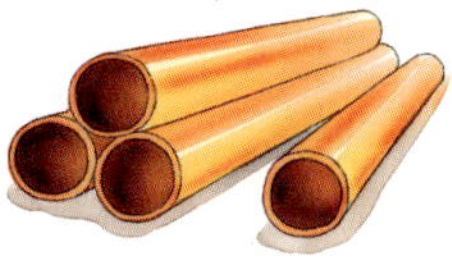
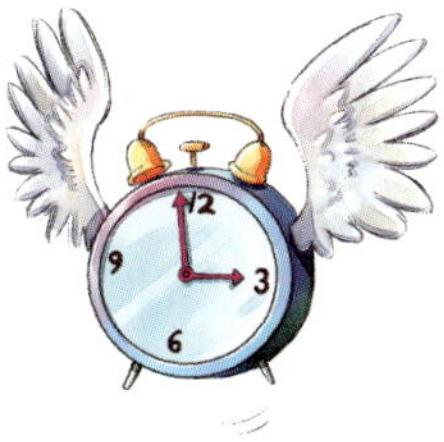

Listen and complete the word. Then match it to the correct picture. **Track 41**

**1** p____   

   h____ **7**

**2** w____   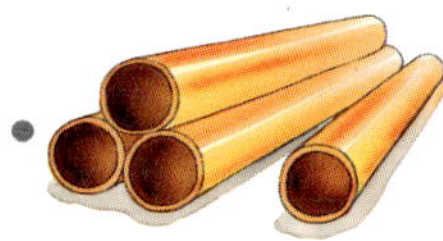

   f____ **8**

**3** t____   

   d____ **9**

**4** b____   

   w____ **10**

**5** d____   

   t____ **11**

**6** r____   

   b____ **12**

# Complete the word for the picture and fill in the puzzle.

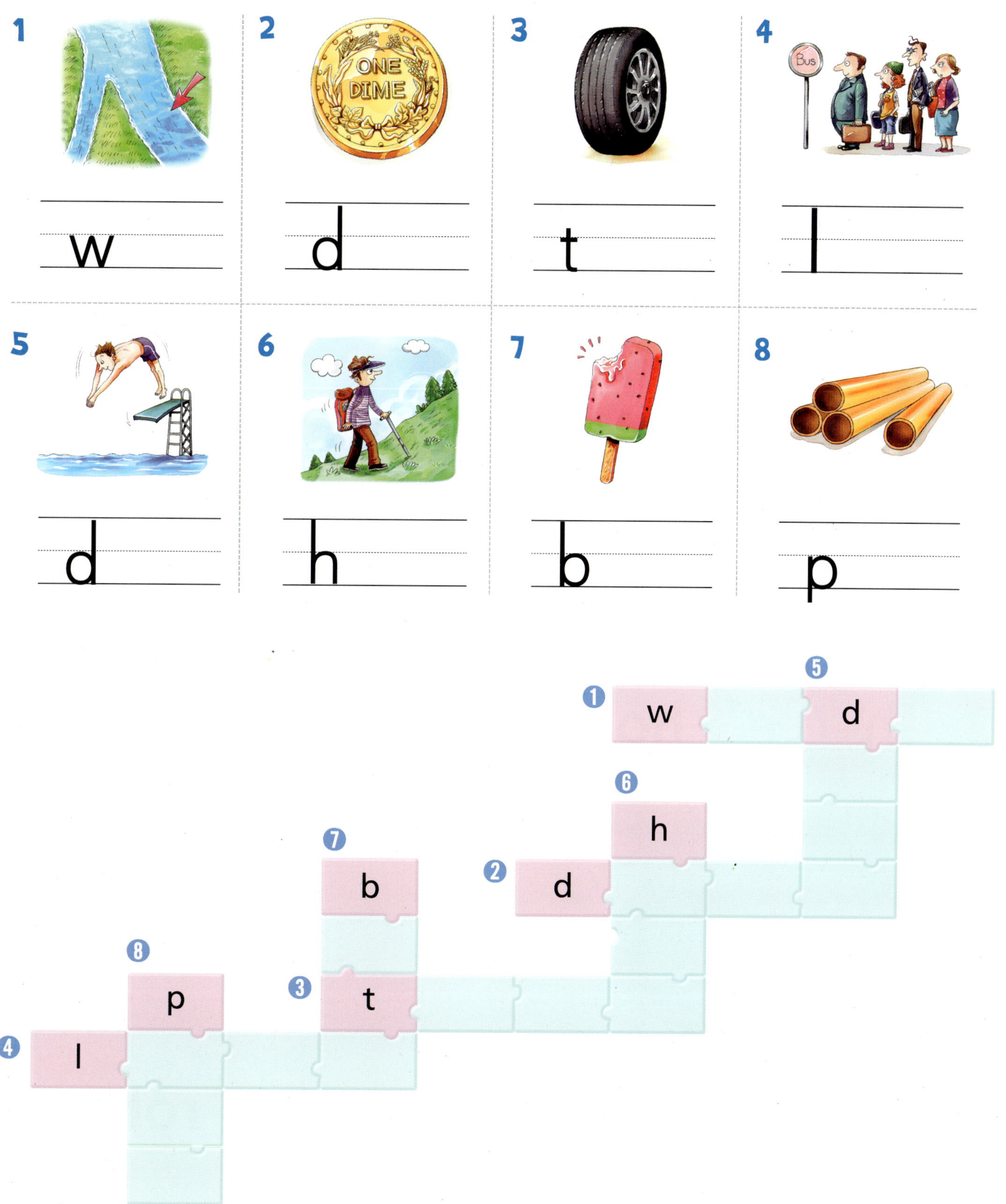

# Long Vowel O

Listen and repeat.  Track 42

o l e → h o l e → h o l e

o b e → g l o b e → g l o b e

Track 43

**-ole**

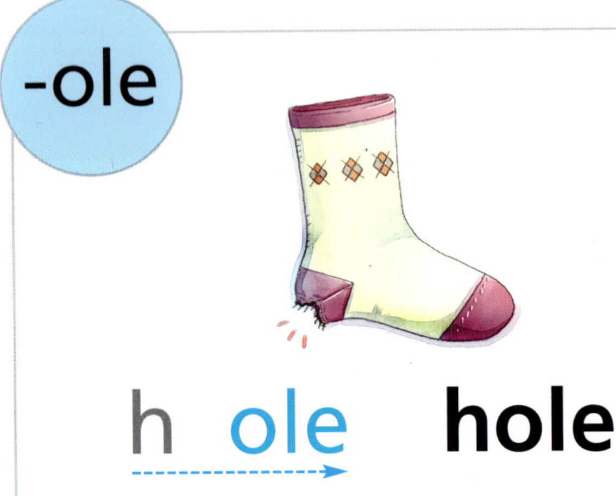

h ole **hole**

m ole **mole**

**-obe**

gl obe **globe**

r obe **robe**

   → 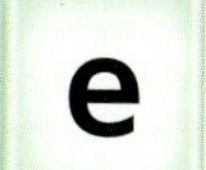  →  

o m e → d o m e → d o m e

o n e → c o n e → c o n e

Track 45

**-ome**

d **ome** **dome**

h **ome** **home**

**-one**

c **one** **cone**

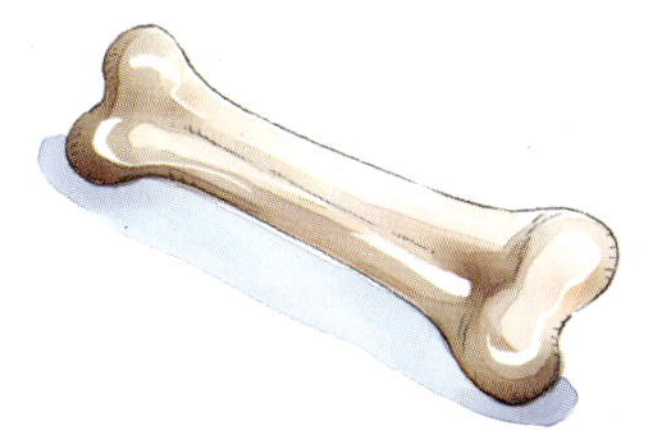

b **one** **bone**

  Track 46

**Read the word and circle the correct picture.**

**1** **hole**

  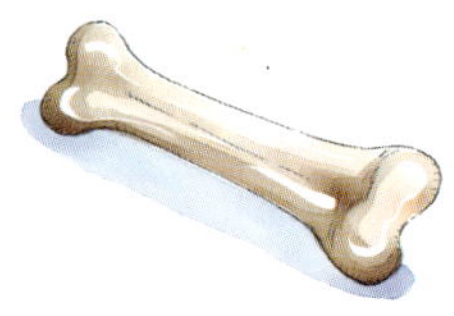

**2** **dome**

**3** **globe**

 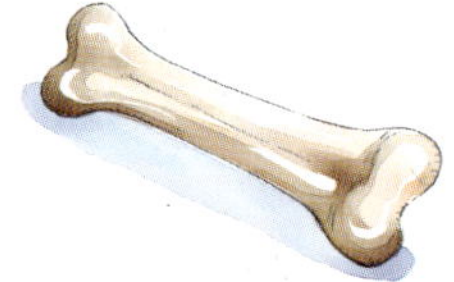 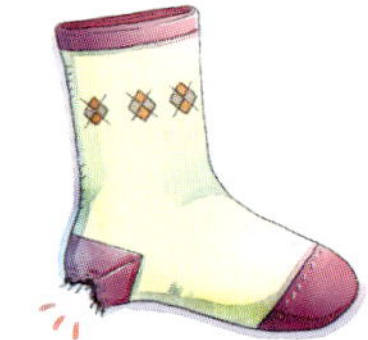

**4** **cone**

**5** **robe**

**6** **home**

Listen to the word and circle the correct picture. Then complete the word. Track 47

**1**

_ _ _ _ m l

**2**

b n

**3**

h m

**4**

r b

**5**

g l b

**6**

c n

Listen to the word and circle the correct picture.  Track 48

Listen and choose the correct word. Then write it. Track 49

home    cone    hole    bone    robe    dome

1 ___________________

2 ___________________

3 ___________________

4 ___________________

## Write the correct word.

**1**

A mouse is in the ___________.

hole | robe

**2**

The man points to Korea on the ___________.

home | globe

**3**

A fish ___________ is on the plate.

bone | mole

**4**

The family all wear ___________ hats.

cone | globe

**5**

The roof of the house is a ___________.

dome | cone

A mole in my garden.

He digs a hole and makes a dome.

He calls it his home.

The mole in his home.

He makes dough and bakes a bone
 with it.

He calls it a bone pie.

The mole and I are in my happy garden.

# Trace and write the words.

**-ole**

hole

mole

**-obe**

globe

robe

**-ome**

dome

home

**-one**

cone

bone

# Long Vowel O

o s e → **h** o s e → **h** o s e

**-ose**

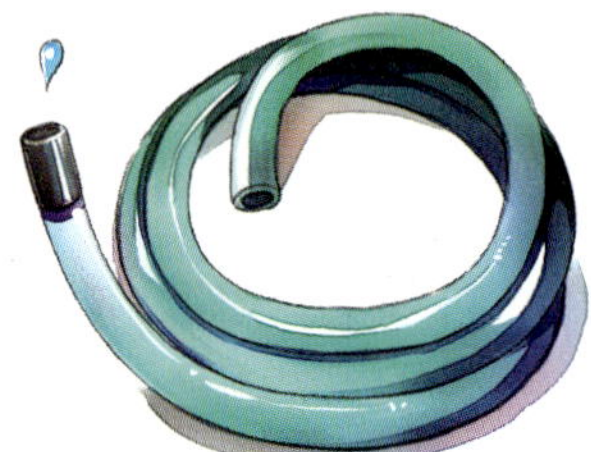

h ose **hose**

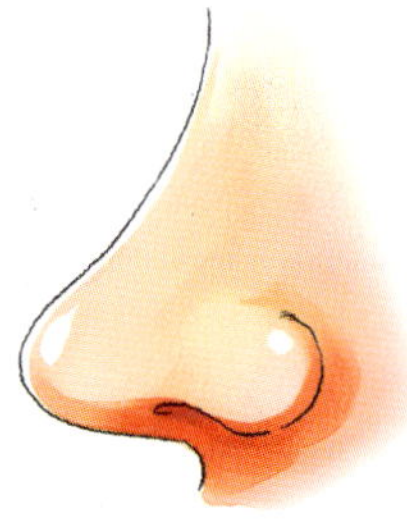

n ose **nose**

p ose **pose**

r ose **rose**

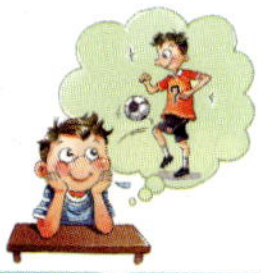

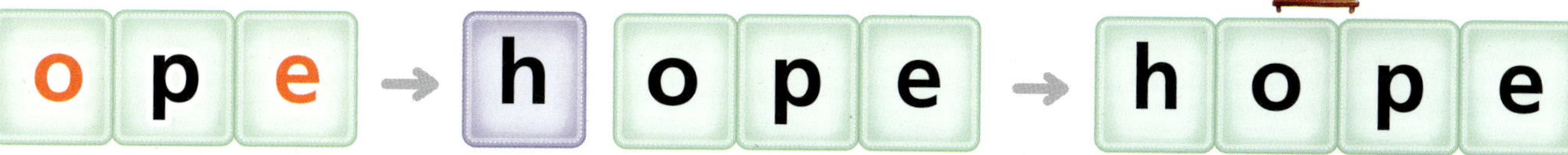

o p e → h o p e → h o p e

o t e → n o t e → n o t e

Track 54

## -ope

h **ope** → **hope**

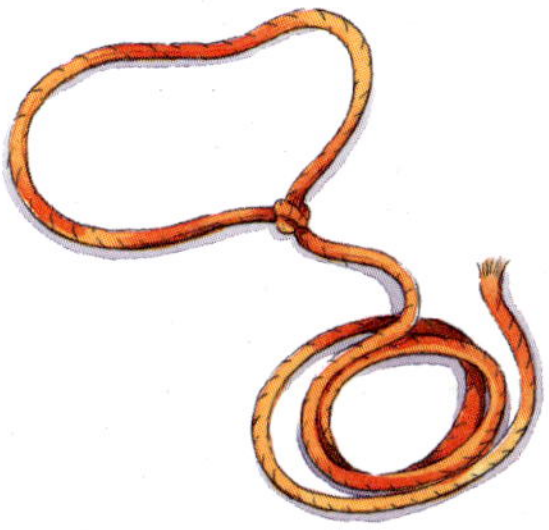

r **ope** → **rope**

## -ote

n **ote** → **note**

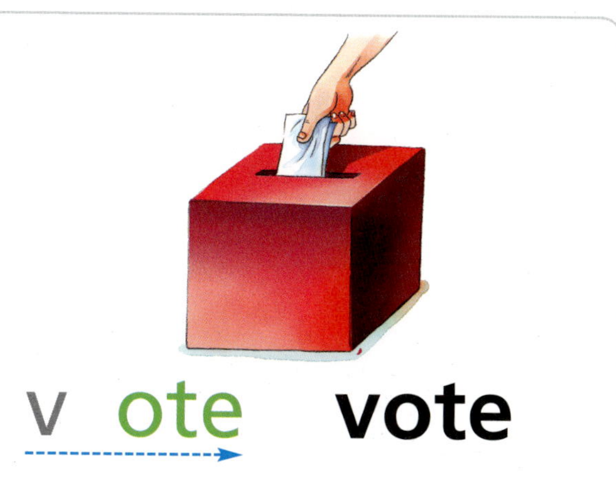

v **ote** → **vote**

Let's chant! Track 55

# Read the word and circle the correct picture.

**1** hose

**2** note

**3** nose

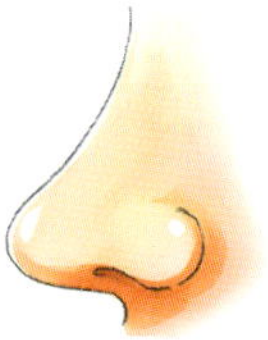

**4** hope

**5** rose

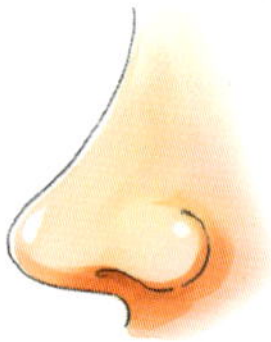

**6** vote

Listen to the word and choose the correct letters. Then write it.



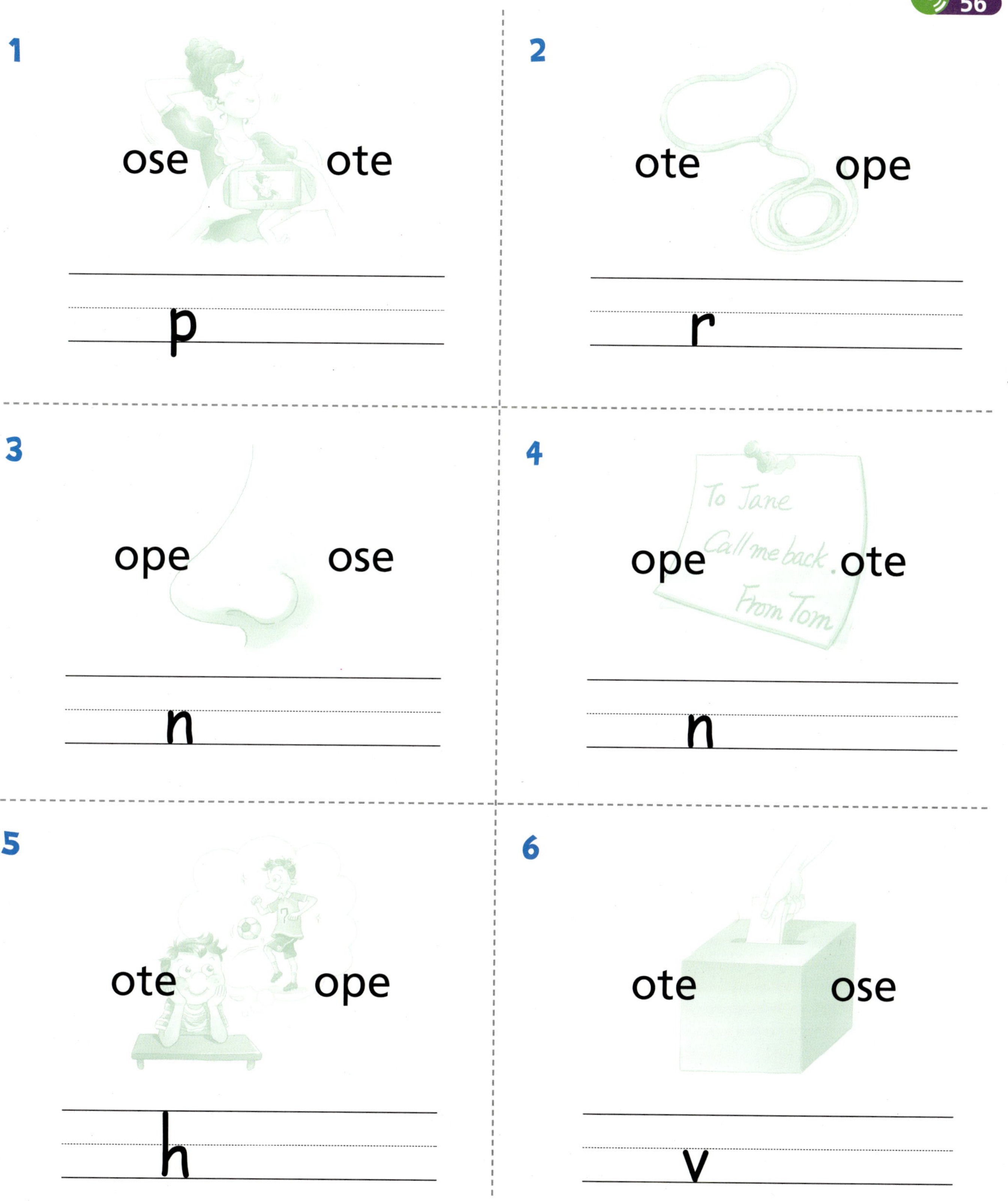

**1**

ose    ote

_____________

p

**2**

ote    ope

_____________

r

**3**

ope    ose

_____________

n

**4**

ope    .ote

_____________

n



**5**

ote    ope

_____________

h

**6**

ote    ose

_____________

v

Listen to the word and circle the correct picture.  Track 57

Listen and choose the correct word. Then write it. Track 58

| rope | note | vote | nose | pose | hope |

1 ______________________

2 ______________________

3 ______________________

4 ______________________

## Write the correct word.

**1**

She smells a ___________.

| rose | hope |

**2**

There is a __________ on the board.

| pose | note |

**3**

The baby's __________ is running.

| vote | nose |

**4**

The man uses a __________ to climb up.

| rope | pose |

**5**

Mom waters the flowers with a __________.

| pose | hose |

# Read Along!

Track 59

I **note** down my dreams.

A model! A model!
I **hope** to be a model.
I can **pose** with a **rose**.

A fireman! A fireman!
I **hope** to be a fireman.
I can water with a **hose**.

Trace and write the words.

**-ose**

hose

nose

pose

rose

**-ope**

hope

rope

**-ote**

note

vote

# Review 3

Match the correct letters to complete the word.

**1**

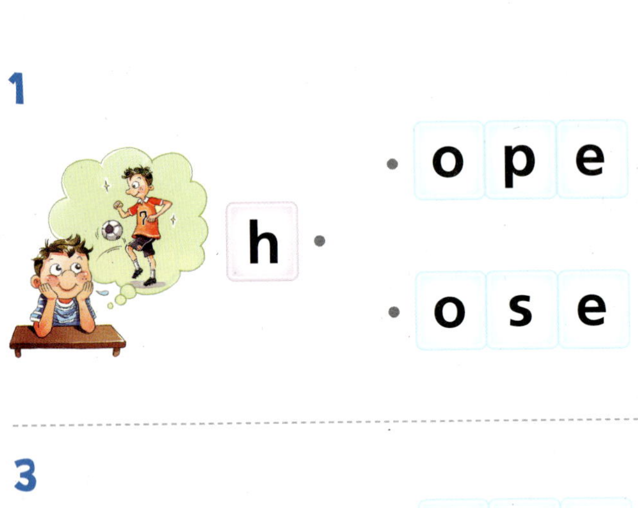

h

- ope
- ose

**2**

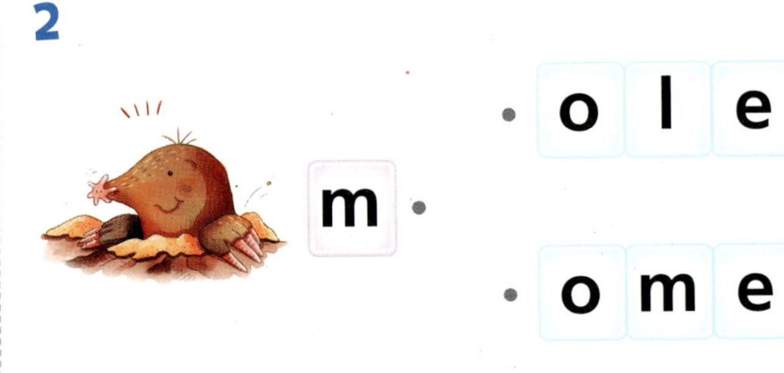

m

- ole
- ome

**3**

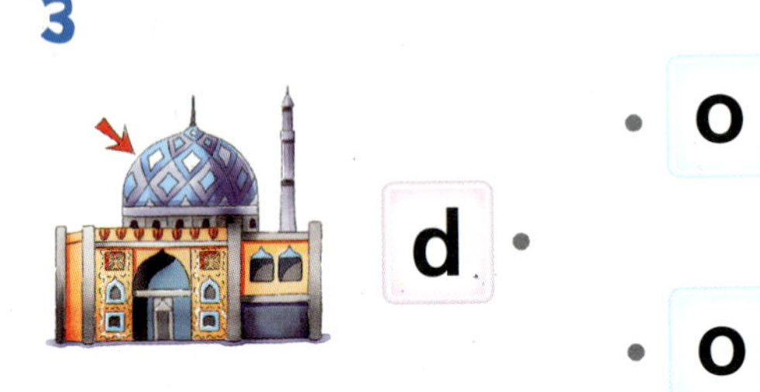

d

- ote
- ome

**4**

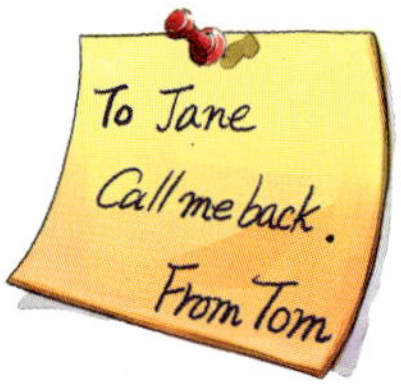

To Jane
Call me back.
From Tom

n

- one
- ote

**5**

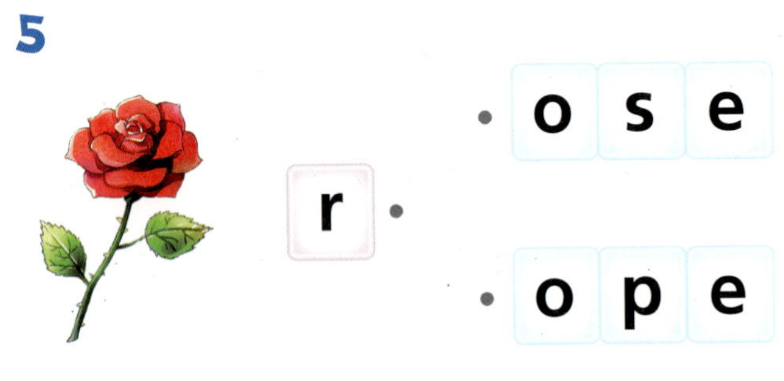

r

- ose
- ope

**6**

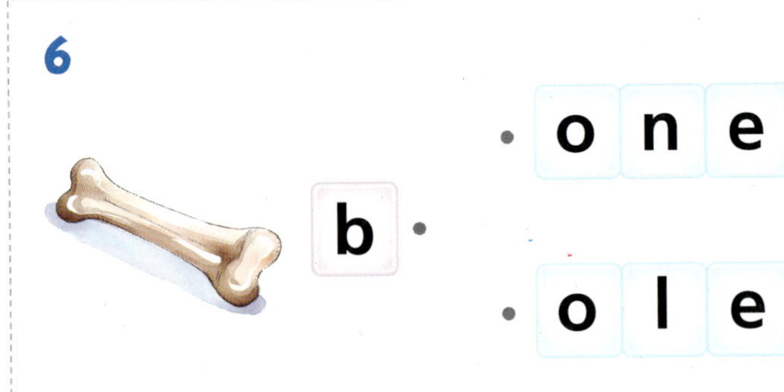

b

- one
- ole

**7**

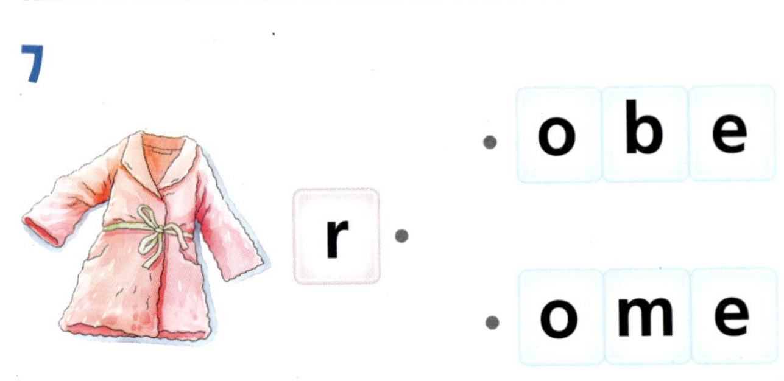

r

- obe
- ome

**8**

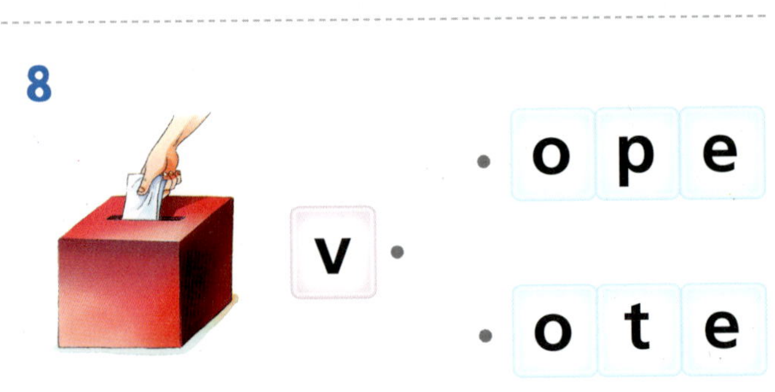

v

- ope
- ote

Listen to the word. Then circle the correct picture and letters.  Track 60

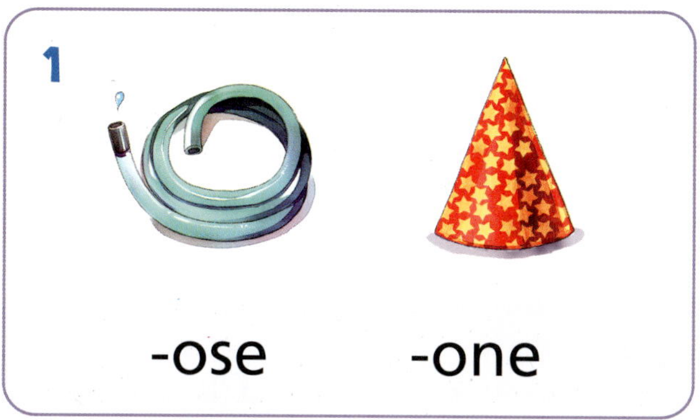

-ose    -one

-ope    -obe

-obe    -ome

-ose    -ole

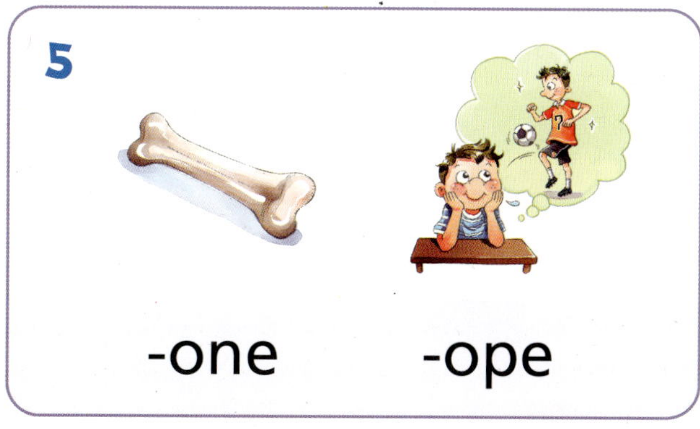

-one    -ope

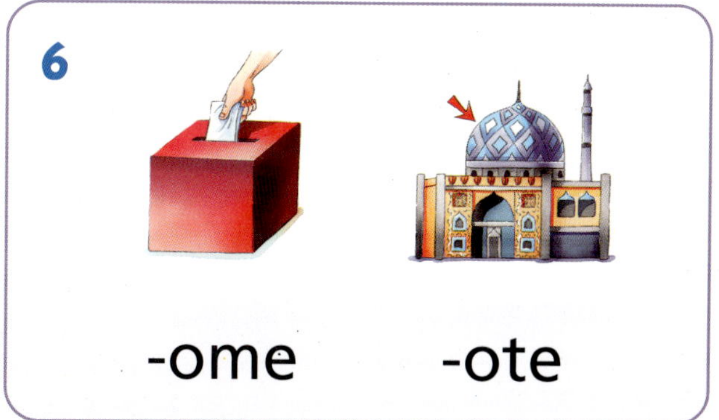

-ome    -ote

-ose    -one

-ole    -ope

Listen and complete the word. Then match it to the correct picture. **Track 61**

**1** h_____

h_____ **7**

**2** c_____

p_____ **8**

**3** n_____

h_____ **9**

**4** d_____

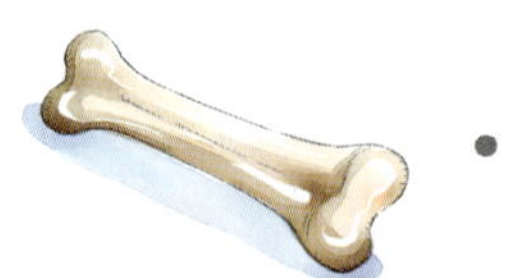

b_____ **10**

**5** r_____

m_____ **11**

**6** r_____

v_____ **12**

64

Listen and connect the correct words. Track 62

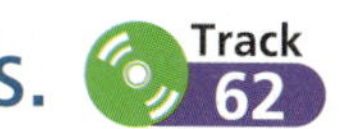

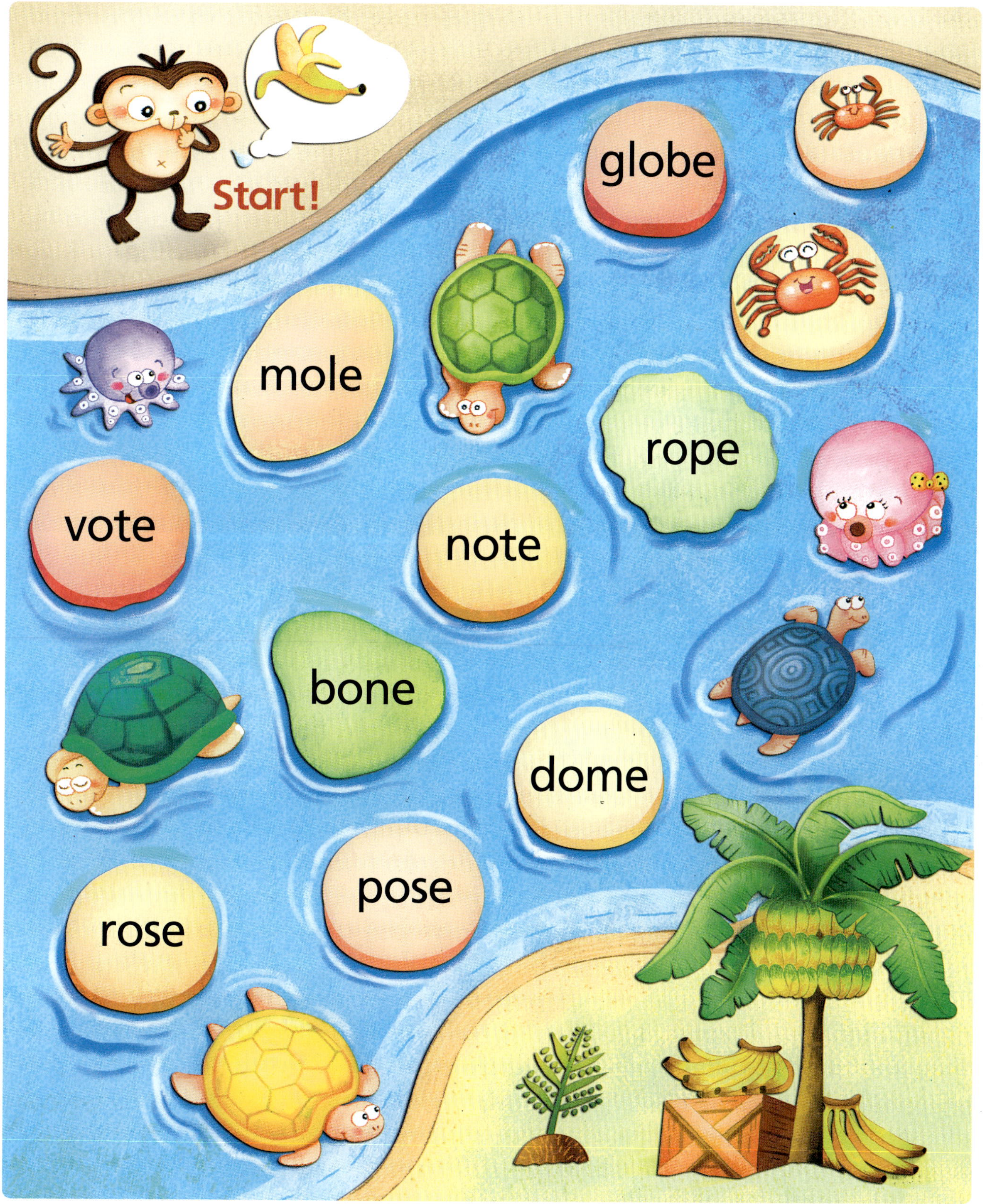

**Listen and repeat.**  Track 63

u n e → d u n e → d u n e

 Track 64

**-une**

d **une**  **dune**

J **une**  **June**

t **une**  **tune**

Listen and repeat. 

**Track 65**

u b e → t u b e → t u b e

u s e → f u s e → f u s e

**Track 66**

**-ube**

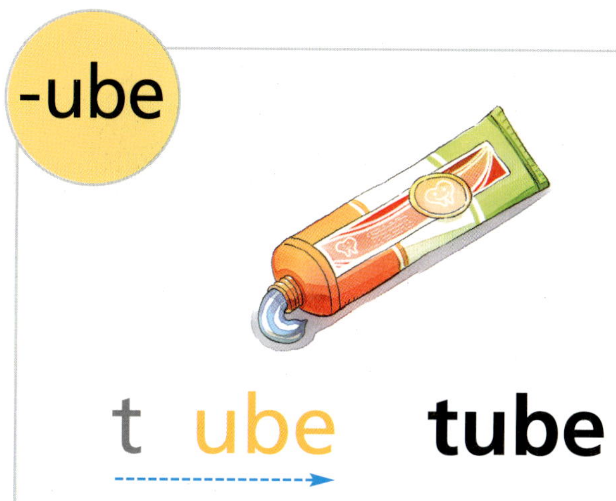

t ube    **tube**

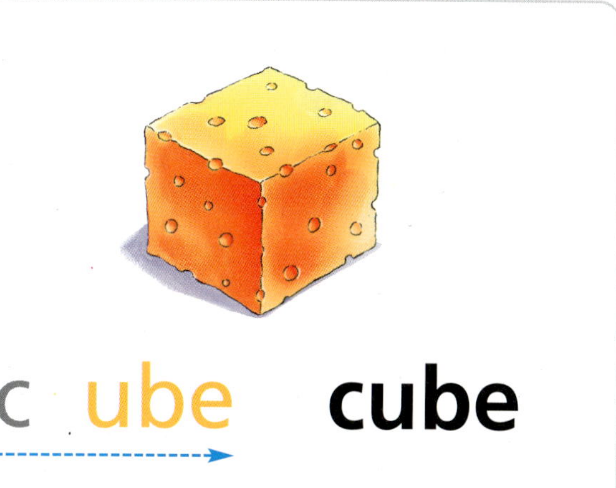

c ube    **cube**

**-use**

f use    **fuse**

**Let's chant!**   **Track 67**

# Circle the picture ending with the given letters.

**1**   -une

**2**   -use

**3**   -une

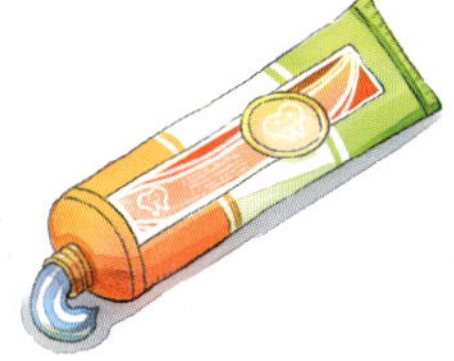  

**4**   -ube

**5**   -une

  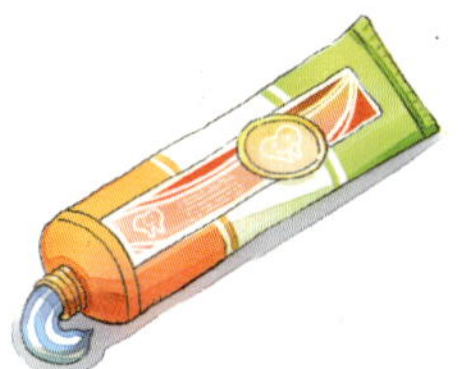

**6**   -ube

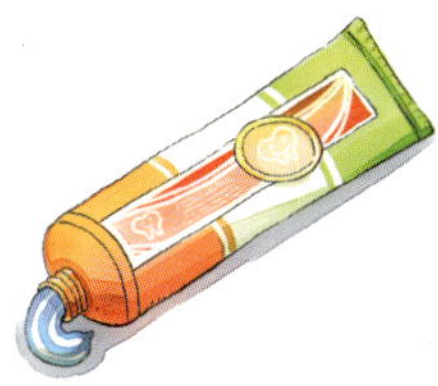  

Listen to the word and circle the correct picture. Then complete the word. **Track 68**

Listen to the word and circle the correct picture. 

Listen to the word and write the missing letters. 

1  t __ b __

2  f __ s __

3  t __ n __

4  c __ __ __

5  J __ __ __

6  d __ __ __

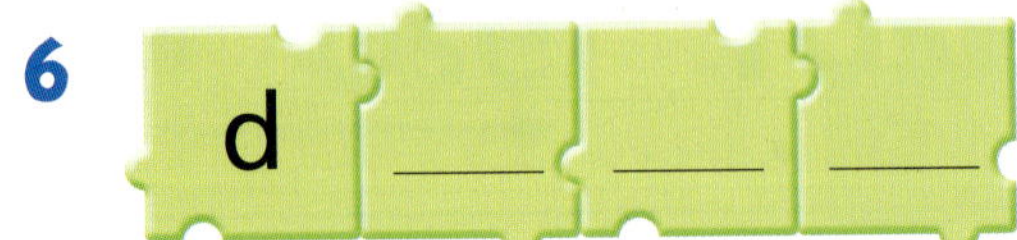

Write the correct letters in the blank. Then choose the correct picture.

**1** A man walks on the d__________ with a camel. ☐

-une  -ube

**2** Jane's birthday is on J__________ 7th. ☐

-use  -une

**3** There are some c__________s on the table. ☐

-ube  -use

**4** He sings out of t__________. ☐

-une  -ube

**5** The light is out. Check the f__________ box. ☐

-ube  -use

a

b

c

d

e

# Read Along!



In the magic land,
  what can you see?
I see a man with a wand on the dune.
A red tube becomes an apple.

In the magic land,
  what can you hear?
I hear a harp tune from the dune.
A colorful cube makes a harp tune.

# Trace and write the words.

**-une**

dune

June

tune

**-ube**

tube

cube

**-use**

fuse

# Long Vowel U

Listen and repeat. 
Track 72

Track 73

**-ure**

**-ule**

Listen and repeat.  Track 74

u t e → c u t e → c u t e

u g e → h u g e → h u g e

 Track 75

**-ute**

c ute  **cute**

m ute  **mute**

**-uge**

h uge  **huge**

**Let's chant!** Track 76

Circle the picture ending with the given letters.

**1** -ure

**2** -uge

**3** -ure

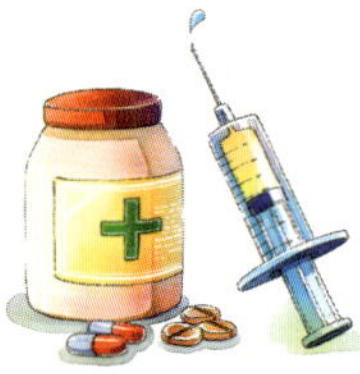

**4** -ute

**5** -ule

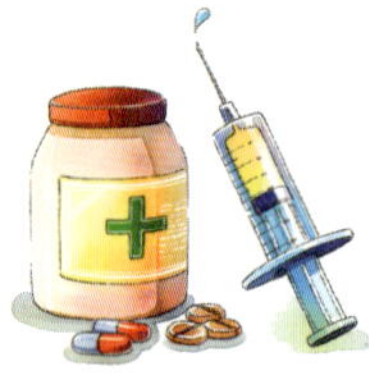

**6** -ute

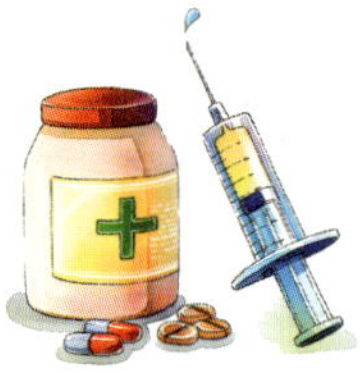

Listen to the word and choose the correct letters. Then write it.



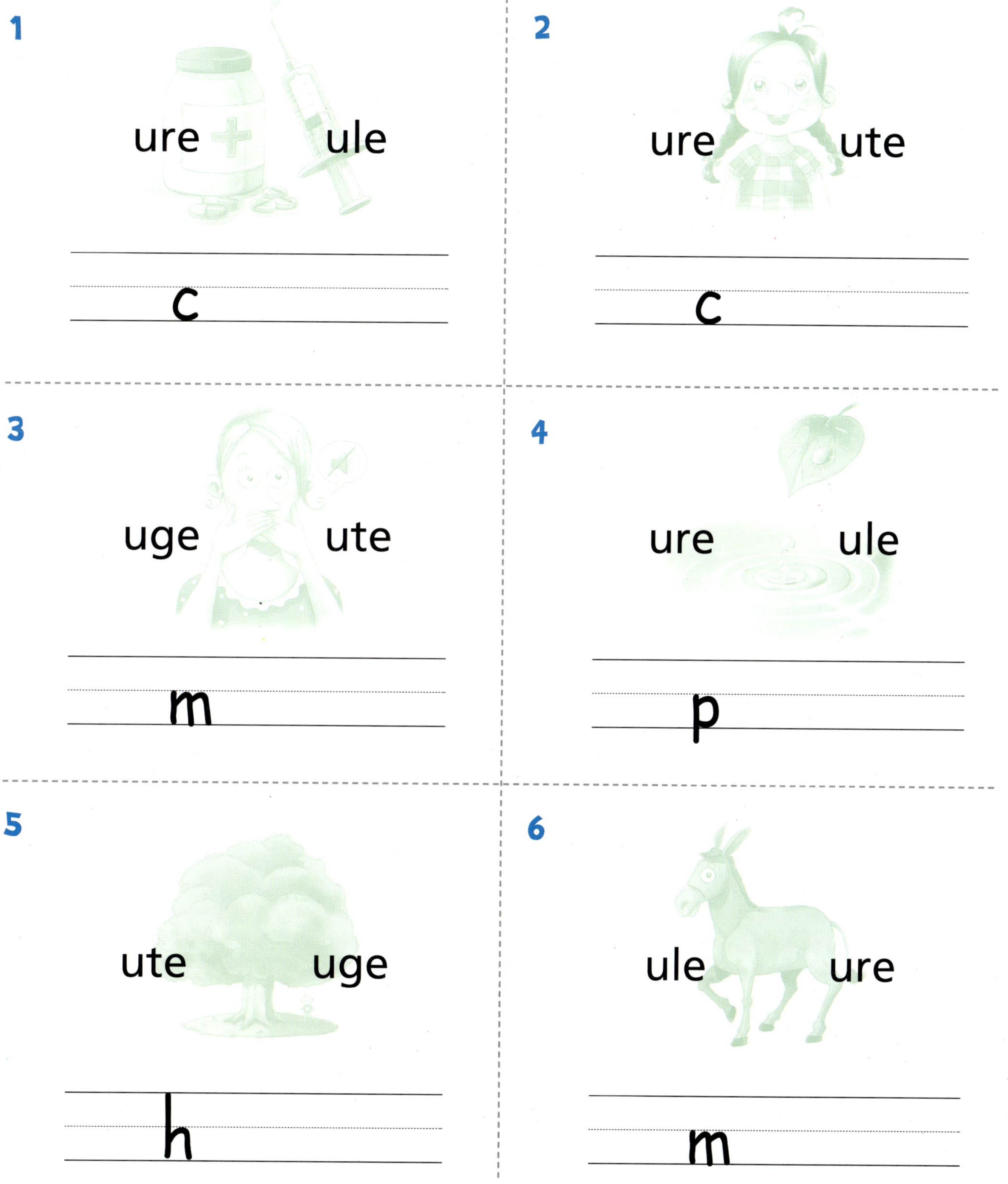

Listen to the word and circle the correct picture. **Track 78**

Listen to the word and write the missing letters. **Track 79**

Write the correct letters in the blank. Then choose the correct picture.

**1** There is a pack on the m__________'s back. ☐
-ute   -ule

**2** There is a h__________ rock in front of the cave. ☐
-ure   -uge

**3** The buttons on the shirt are c__________. ☐
-ute   -ure

**4** This snow is p__________ white. ☐
-ure   -ule

**5** The boy needs a c__________ for his illness. ☐
-ute   -ure

a

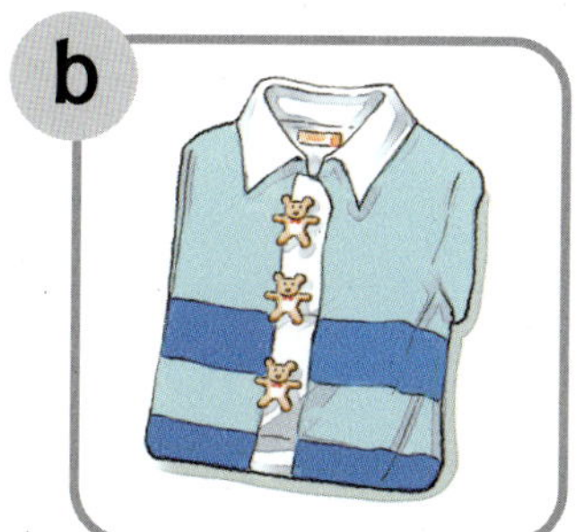
b

c

d

e

# Read Along!

Track 80

Hue is a dancing mule.

He moves his body side to side.

Oh! He is huge, but he is cute.


Sue is a singing swan.

She sings a song loud and clear.

Oh! She is sweet and

her voice is pure.

# Trace and write the words.

**-ure**

cure

pure

**-ule**

mule

**-ute**

cute

mute

**-uge**

huge

# Review 4

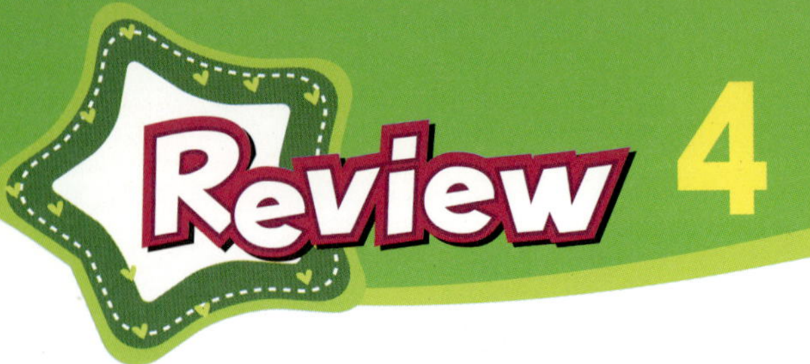

Match the correct letters to complete the word.

1

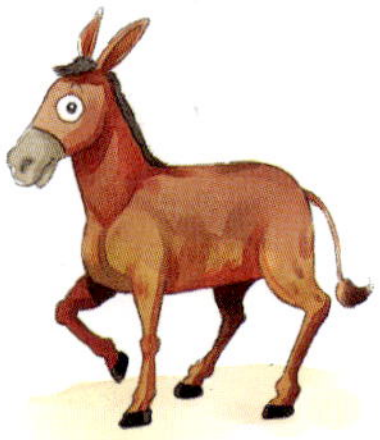

m

- u l e
- u t e

2

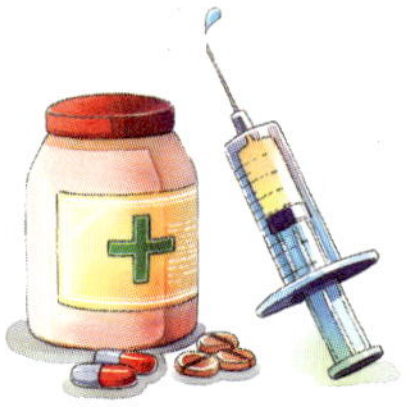

c

- u g e
- u r e

3

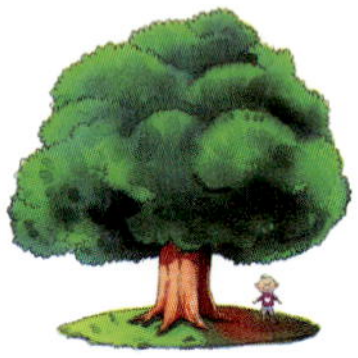

h

- u s e
- u g e

4

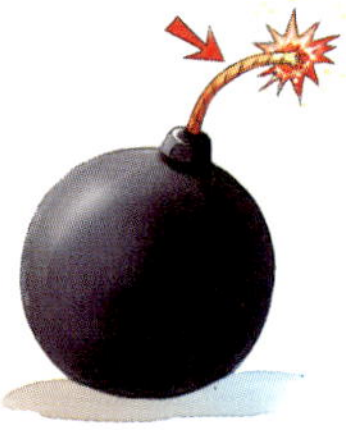

f

- u s e
- u b e

5

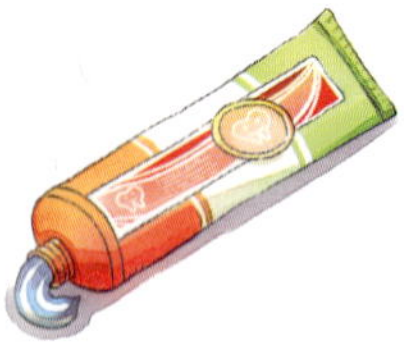

t

- u b e
- u r e

6

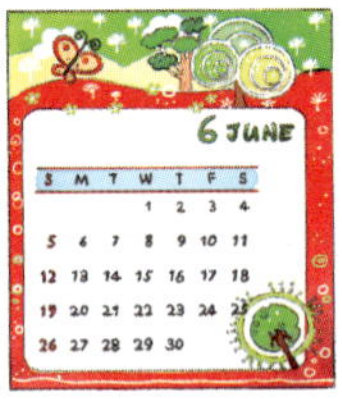


J

- u n e
- u t e

7

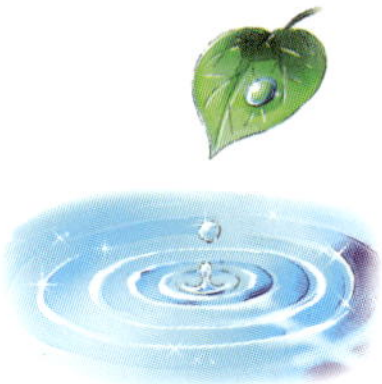

p

- u g e
- u r e

8

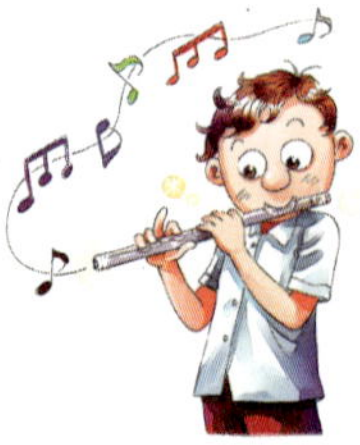

t

- u b e
- u n e

Listen to the word. Then circle the correct picture and letters. **Track 81**

**1**

-uge    -ule

**2**

-ure    -ute

**3**
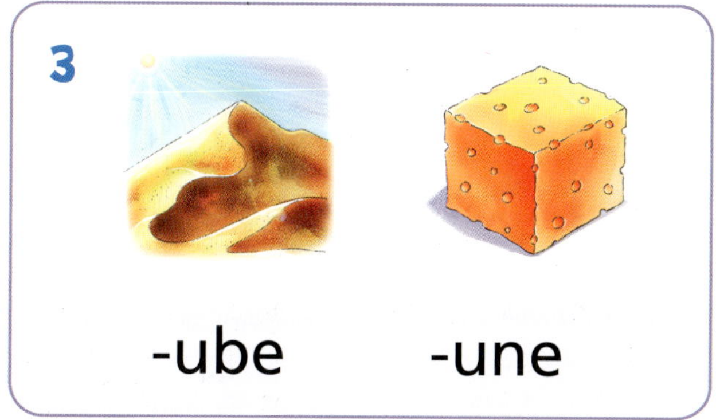

-ube    -une

**4**
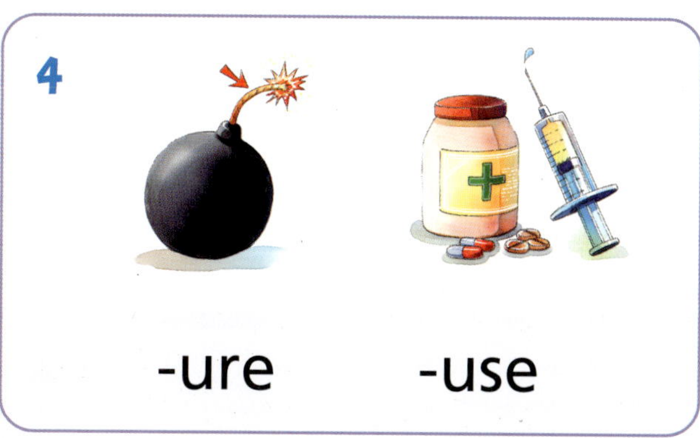

-ure    -use

**5**

-une    -ule

**6**

-ute    -une

**7**

-ube    -ure

**8**

-ule    -ure

Listen and complete the word. Then match it to the correct picture. **Track 82**

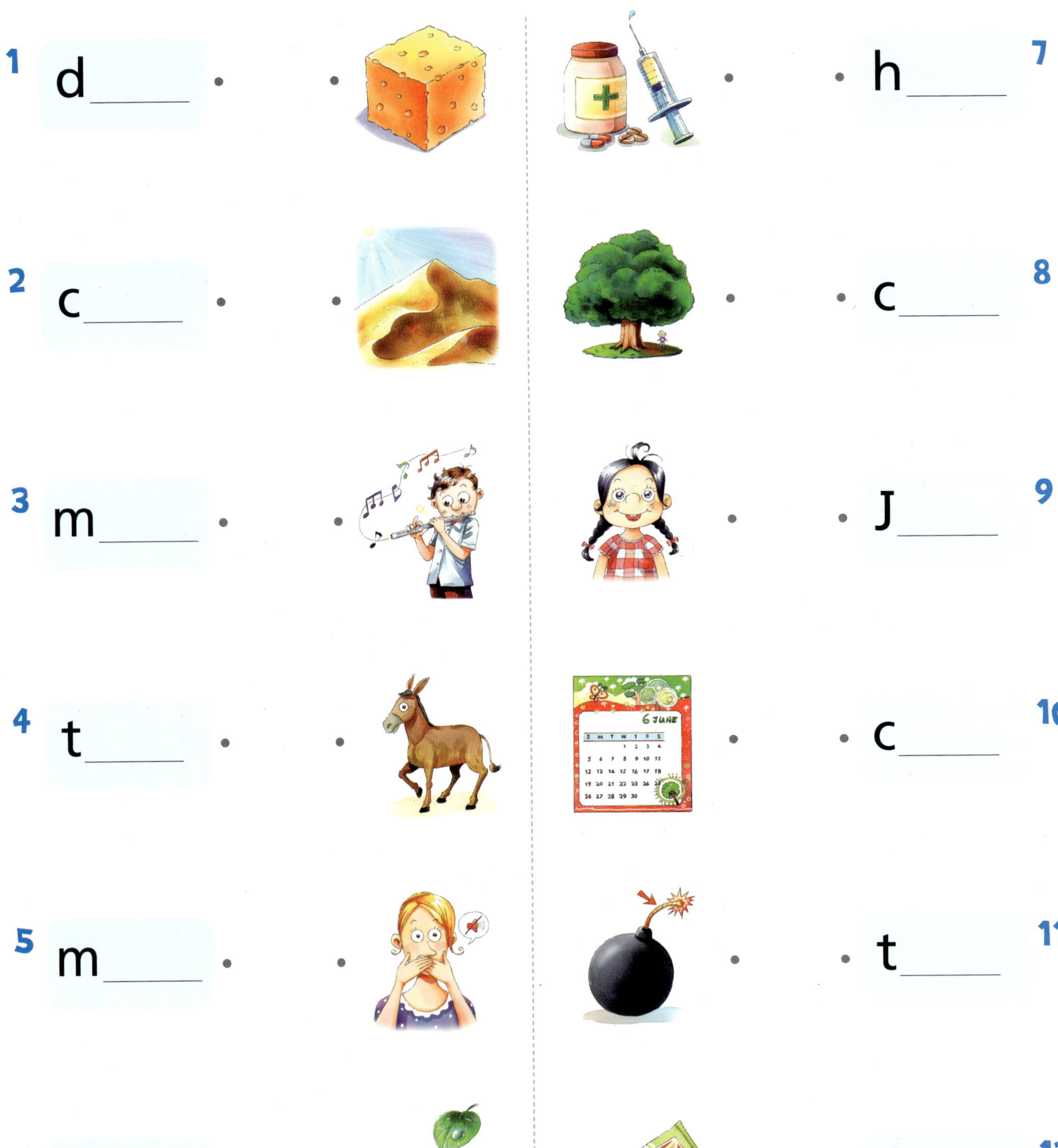

**1** d____

**2** c____

**3** m____

**4** t____

**5** m____

**6** p____

**7** h____

**8** c____

**9** J____

**10** c____

**11** t____

**12** f____

Find the given words in the puzzle. Then write the correct word for the picture.

**Words**   cube   fuse   tune   dune   cute   mule   pure   huge

| t | d | s | f | t | a |
|---|---|---|---|---|---|
| k | u | c | u | b | e |
| o | n | n | s | x | s |
| c | e | a | e | p | e |
| m | u | l | e | u | n |
| b | c | t | x | r | z |
| h | u | g | e | e | w |

**1**

**2**

**3**

**4**

**5**

**6**

**7**

**8**

Listen to the word and check the correct picture. Then fill in the letter circles. **Track 83**

**1**

f  l  a  k  e  k  l  t

**2**

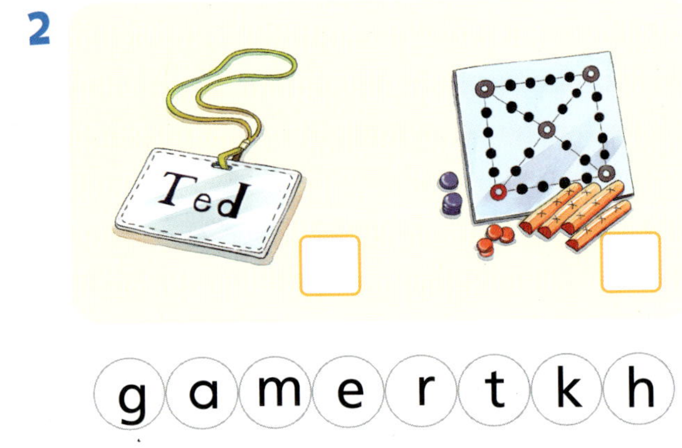

g  a  m  e  r  t  k  h

**3**

g  r  w  c  t  i  m  e

**4**

n  j  p  o  s  e  l  m

**5**

k  d  u  n  e  h  y  v

**6**

s  g  w  f  p  u  r  e

Listen, circle and write the correct word for the picture.

Track 84

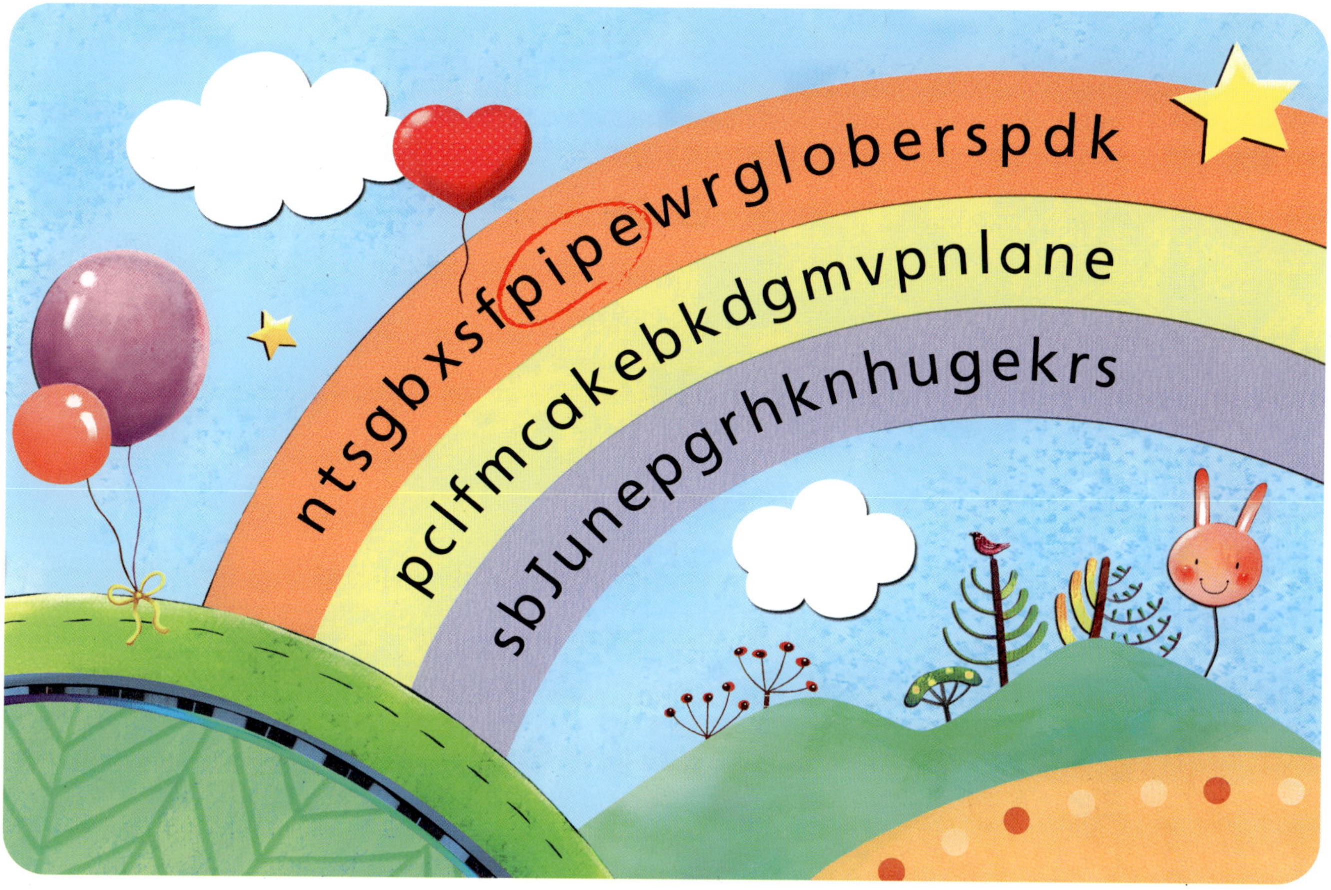

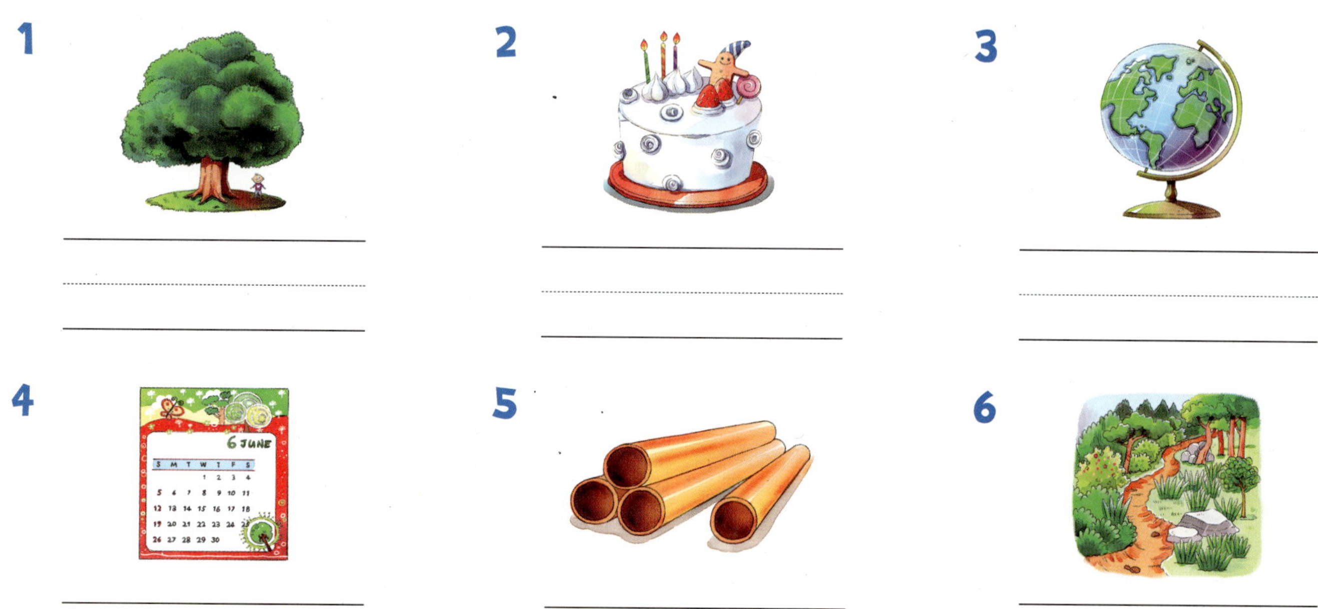

1

2

3

4

5

6

## Match the picture to the correct letters. Then write the word.

**1** 
_______________

**2**
_______________

**3**
_______________

**4**
_______________

**5**
_______________

- -ake -
- -ave -
- -ope -
- -ine -
- -ure -
- -ame -
- -ite -
- -ose -
- -une -
- -age -

**6** 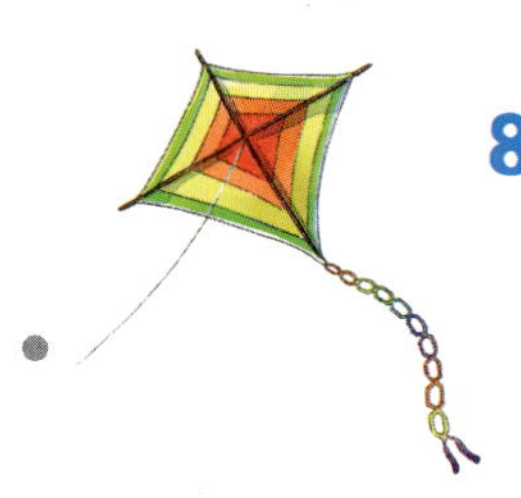
_______________

**7** 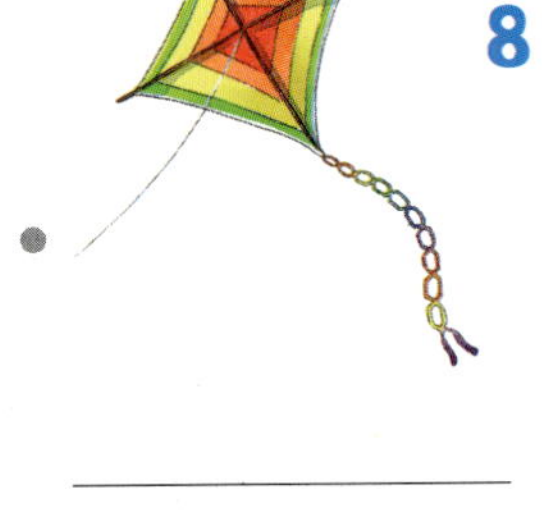
_______________

**8** 
_______________

**9**
_______________

**10** 
_______________

# Look at the picture and check the correct sentence.

**1** 

☐ The children play a game of dice.

☐ The children write their names on the books.

**2** 

☐ The blue cone is on the man's head.

☐ The fish bone is in the large bowl.

**3** 

☐ A mole drinks some water.

☐ A mule eats some carrots.

**4** 

☐ A girl opens the cage.

☐ A girl hides in the cave.

**5** 

☐ The camel rests on the dune.

☐ The camel walks to the lake.

# Let's read the story



**1**

**2**

✓ Check the pictures, referring to the words from the story.

**3**

"What can we get for a dime?"
How about a bike so we can hike?
Nay, we will fall in a hole.

**4**

"What can we get for a dime?"
How about a rake?
Why?
So we can rake for more dimes!

Let's play a game
Start!
u_e
o_e
a_e
i_e
u_e
o_e
a_e
Move forward
2 steps.
i_e
a_e
o_e
u_e
i_e
a_e
u_e
o_e
Move back
2 steps.
How to play
Step 1 Roll the dice and go the correct number of
spaces. Say the word with the given long vowel.
Step 2 If you land on the space with a sentence,
read it and follow the instruction.
Step 3 If you get to the 'Finish!' first, you win the game.

Move forward
3 steps.
Move back
5 steps.
i_e
u_e
o_e
a_e
a_e
o_e
u_e
i_e
a_e
o_e
u_e
i_e
o_e
a_e
i_e
Move forward
6 steps.
u_e
o_e
a_e
i_e
u_e
o_e
a_e
i_e
u_e
Finish!
a_e
o_e
Move back
1 step.

Listen to the word and check the correct word. 

**e.g.**

 ① lake ✓ bake ③ rake

**1**

 ① hole ② globe ③ robe

**2**

 ① nose ② pose ③ hose

**3**

 ① tune ② June ③ dune

**4**

 ① tube ② fuse ③ cube

**5**

 ① dome ② cone ③ home

# Listen to the word and check the correct word for the picture.

Track 87

**e.g.**

✓ 1   ② 2   ③ 3

**6**

① 1   ② 2   ③ 3

**7**

① 1   ② 2   ③ 3

**8**

① 1   ② 2   ③ 3

**9**

① 1   ② 2   ③ 3

**10**

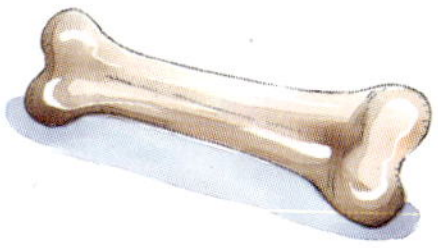

① 1   ② 2   ③ 3

# Listen to the word and write the missing letters. 

Track 88

e.g.

 p i n e

**11**  o □ e

**12**  a □ e

**13**  u □ e

**14**  i □ e

**15**  o □ e

**16**  u □ e

**17**  a □ e

**18**  i □ e

**19**  i □ e

**20**  a □ e

Look at the picture and check the correct word.

**e.g.**

❶ bone    ✓ hose    ❸ hole

**21**

❶ cane    ❷ wide    ❸ cone

**22**

❶ tire    ❷ dome    ❸ huge

**23**

❶ vote    ❷ mole    ❸ June

**24**

❶ fuse    ❷ rope    ❸ bone

**25**

❶ vase    ❷ cage    ❸ bake

# Check the picture ending with the given letters.

**e.g.** | -ite

**26** | -one

**27** | -ape

**28** | -ole

**29** | -ure

**30** | -ave

Read and write the correct words.

**e.g.**

A woman __wipe__s a __vase__ with a cloth.

bake wipe game vase

**31**

A girl _________s to get a chocolate _________.

cake bone hope hike

**32**

_________ bears are in the _________.

dive five cave nose

**33**

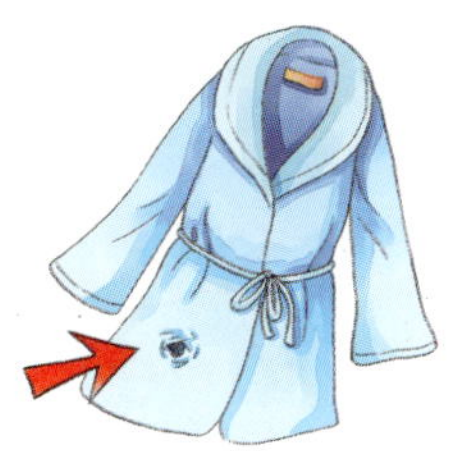

There is a small _________ on the _________.

dune cute robe hole

**34**

The man puts a _________ out with a _________.

fire home hose tire

# Glossary

## Unit 1 | ake · ape · ave

 cake

 lake

 bake

 rake

 cape

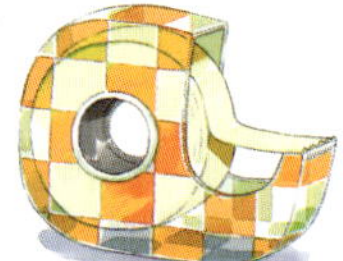 tape

 cave

 wave

## Unit 2 | ame · ane · age · ase

 name

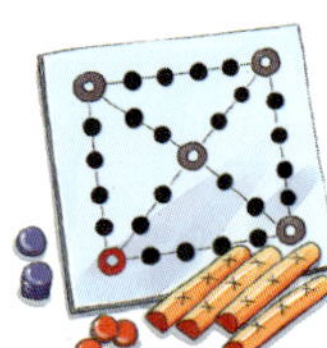 game

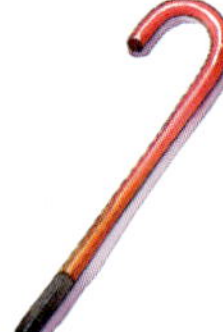 cane

 lane

 cage

 page

 base

 vase

bike

hike

dime

time

pine

line

kite

bite

## Unit 4 | ide · ipe · ire · ive

ride

wide

pipe

wipe

fire

tire

five

dive

# Glossary



## Unit 5 | ole · obe · ome · one

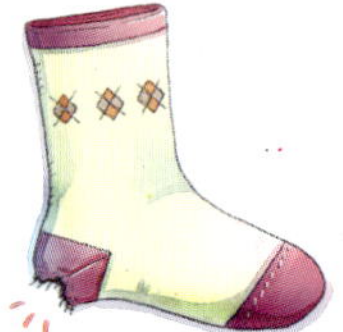

hole

mole

globe

robe

dome

home

cone

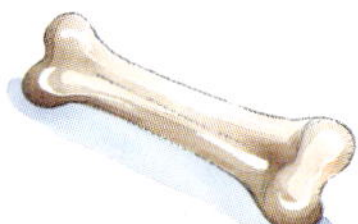

bone

## Unit 6 | ose · ope · ote

hose

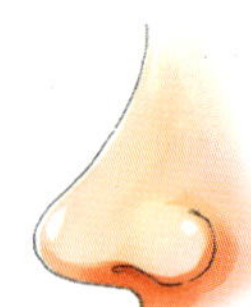

nose

pose

rose

hope

rope

note

vote

dune

June

tune

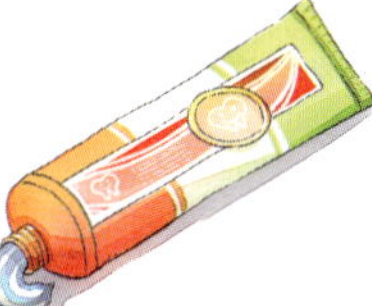

tube

cube

fuse



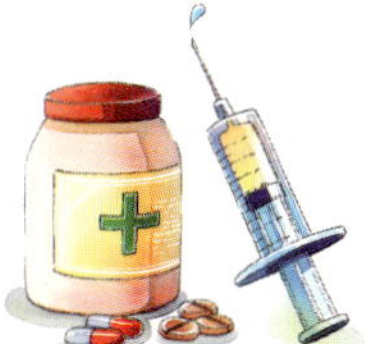

cure

pure

mule

cute

mute

huge

Phonics
Wonder

# Phonics Wonder

LEVEL 3

Long Vowels

## Workbook

Young & Son Global, Inc.

# Phonics Wonder

**LEVEL 3**

## Long Vowels

## Workbook

YSG Young & Son Global, Inc.

# Contents

# Long Vowel a

Look and circle the correct ending letters.

**1)** 

ape  (ake)

**2)** ape  ave

**3)**  ake  ave

**4)**  ake  ape

**5)** 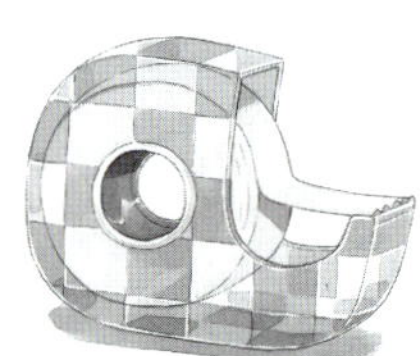 ave  ape

**6)**  ave  ake

Trace and write.

| **-ake** | cake  lake  bake  rake |
| **-ape** | cape        tape |
| **-ave** | cave        wave |

4

# Match and make the word. Then write it.

**1**

w ·

**2**

· l ·   · ake

**3**

· b ·

**4**

· c ·   · ave

**5**

· r ·

**6**

· t ·   · ape

take

Circle the picture with the same ending letters.

**1**

**2**

**3**

Circle the correct word.

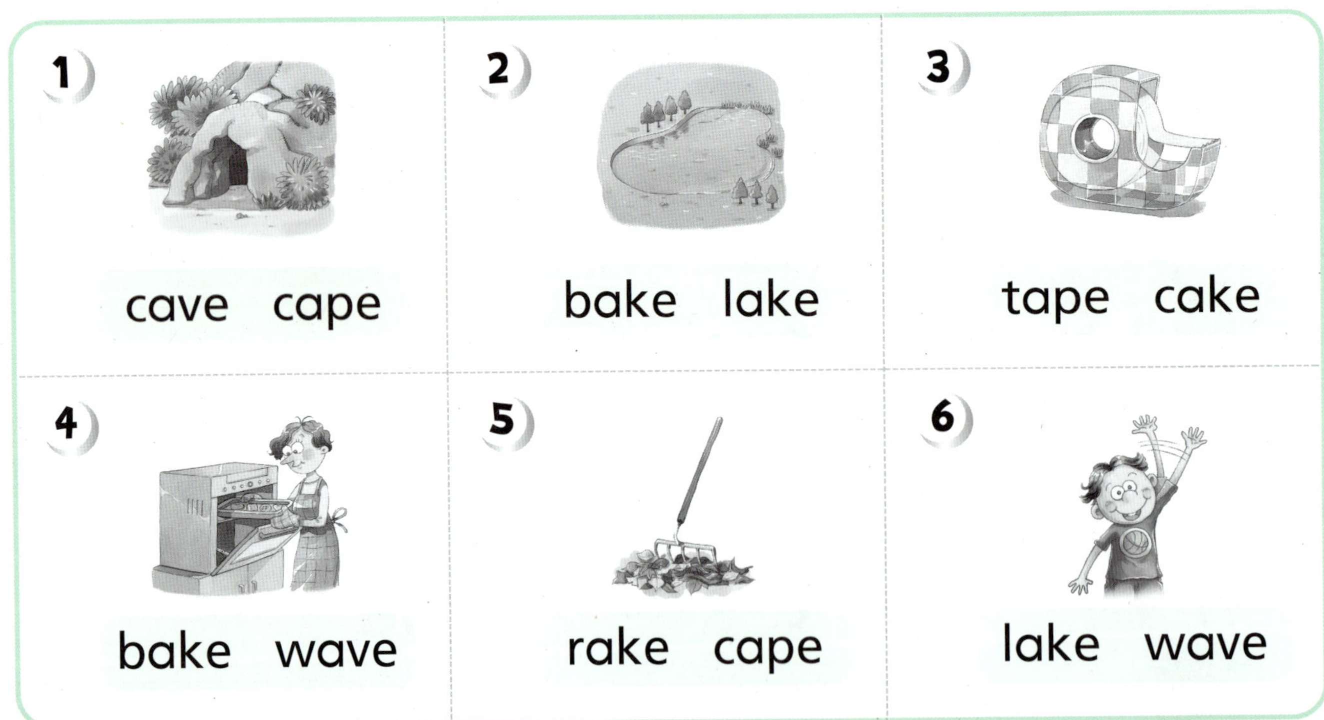

# Look and write the word.

**1** c | ake    cake cake

**2** l | ake

**3** b | ake

**4** r | ake

**5** c | ape

**6** t | ape

**7** c | ave

**8** w | ave

# Long Vowel a

Look and circle the correct ending letters.

**1)** 

ase    ame

**2)**

ane    ame

**3)** 

age    ane

**4)** 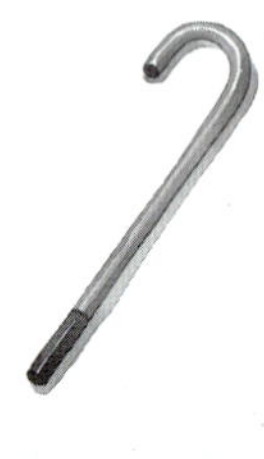

ane    ase

**5)** 

age    ame

**6)** 

ame    ase

Trace and write.

| -ame | name | game |
| -ane | cane | lane |
| -age | age | page |
| -ase | base | vase |

# Match and make the word. Then write it.

**1** 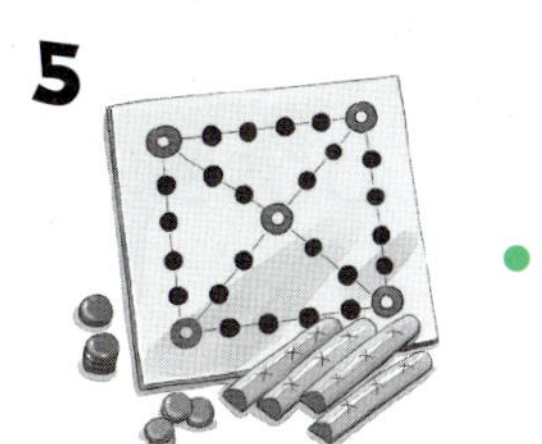

**c**

**ame**

**2**

**g**

**3**

**n**

**age**

**4**

**p**

**5**

**ane**

**v**

**6**

**c**

**ase**

Circle the picture with the same ending letters.

Circle the correct word.

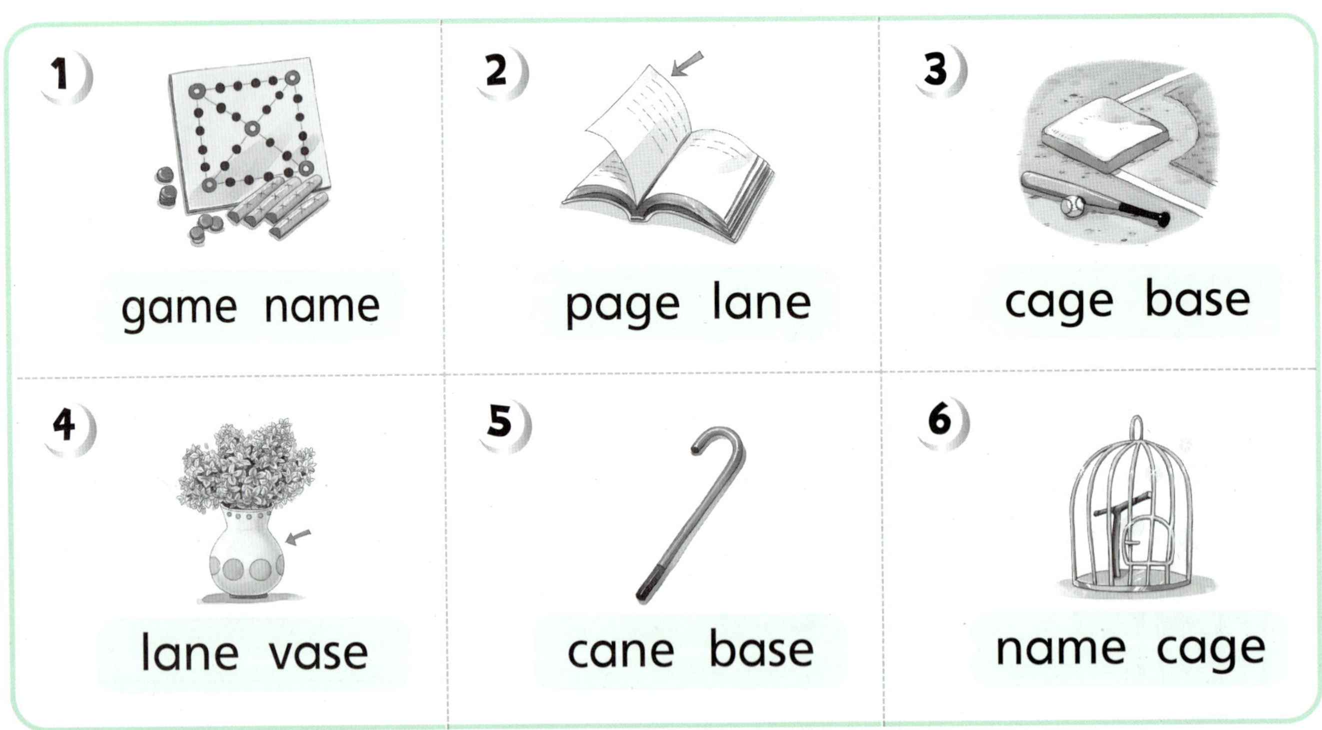

# Look and write the word.

**1** name

**2** game

**3** cane

**4** lane

**5** cage

**6** page

**7** base

**8** vase

# Review 1

Look and circle the correct word.

**1**

cane
cape
rake

**2**

cake
tape
page

**3**

vase
cave
name

**4**

wave
cage
lane

Look and circle the correct picture.

**1** rake

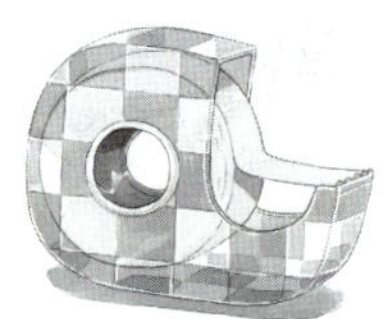

**2** wave

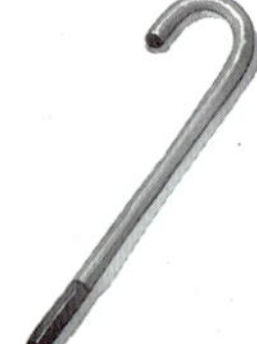

**3** page

## Match and make the word. Then write it.

**1**

v •        • ave

**2**
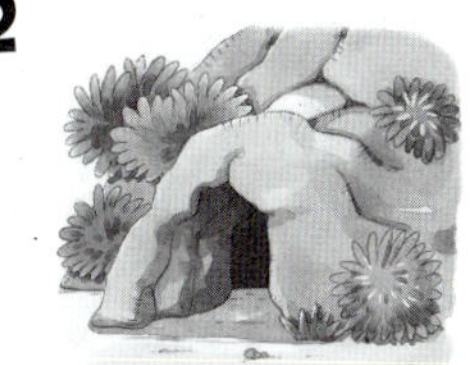
c •        • ane

**3**

l •        • ake

**4**
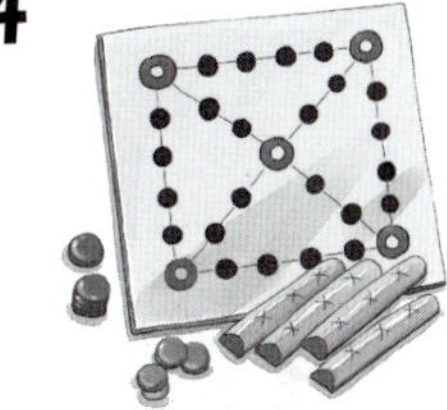
g •        • ase

**5**

p •        • ame

**6**
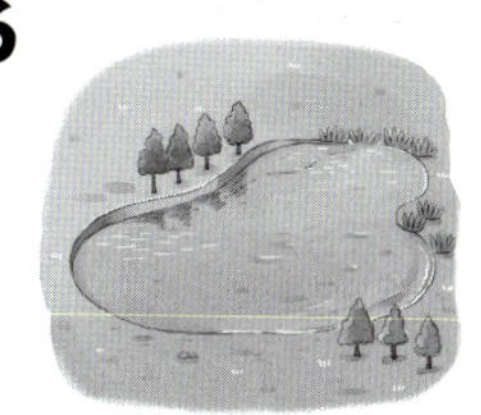
l •        • age

Circle the correct word and write it.

**1)**

name
page

name

**2)**

lake
rake

**3)**

cage
cave

**4)**

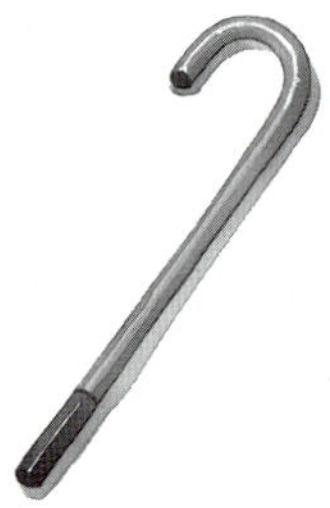

cake
cane

**5)**

cage
bake

**6)**

wave
vase

**7)**

cape
game

**8)**

rake
lane

# Long Vowel a

## Circle the picture with the same ending letters.

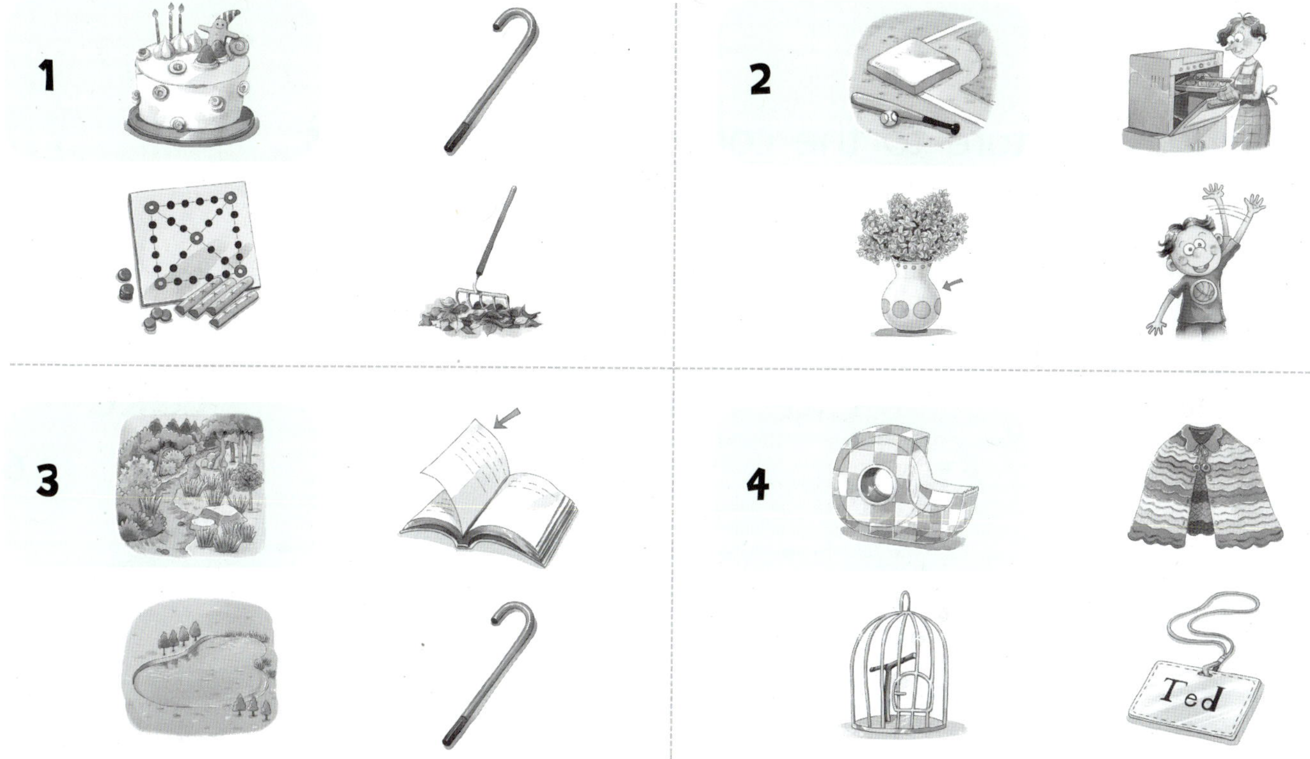

## Look and write the word.

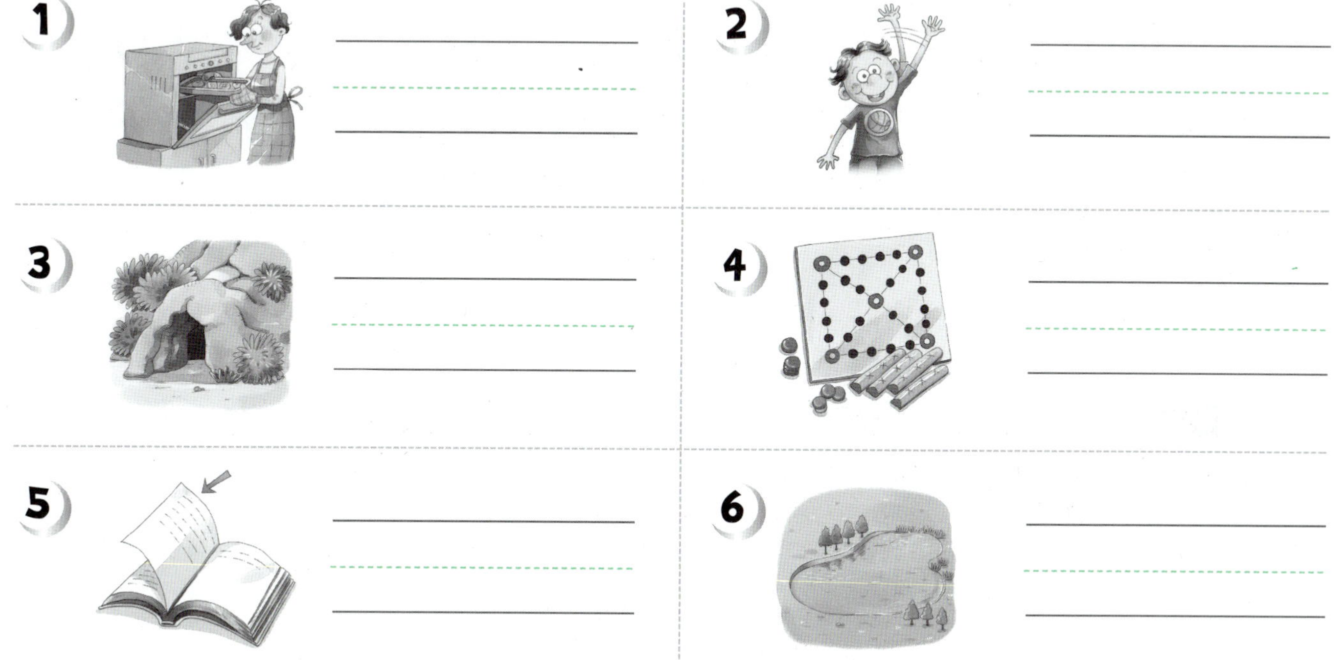

# Long Vowel i

Match the picture to the correct ending letters.

1 

5 

- **-ike** -

2 

6 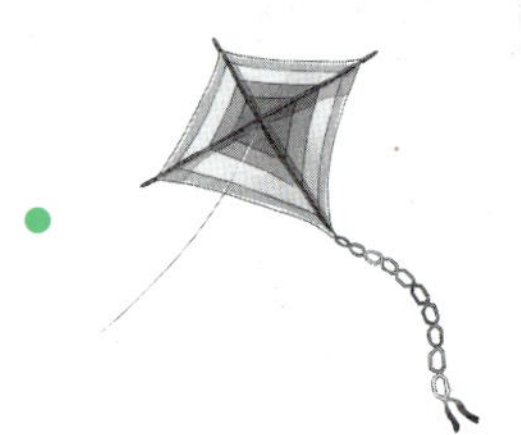

- **-ine** -

3 

7 

- **-ime** -

4 

8 

- **-ite** -

Trace and write.

-ike 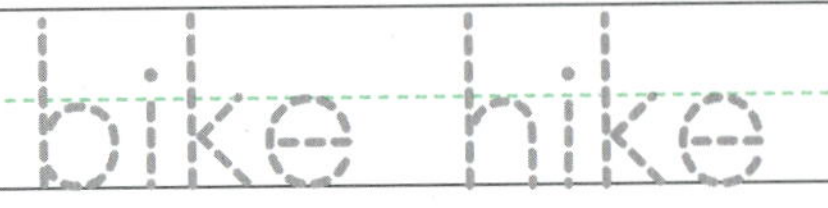


-ime 

-ine 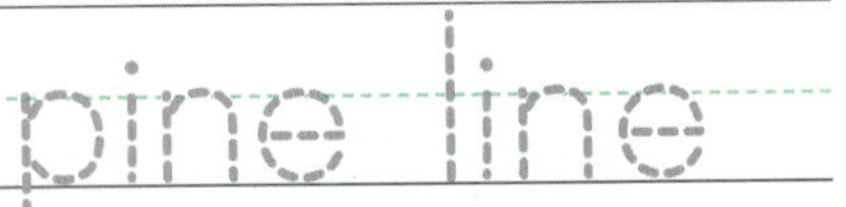


-ite 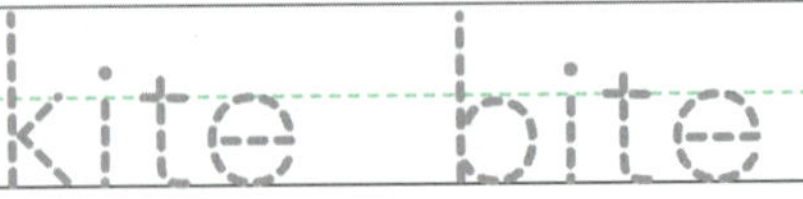

# Match and make the word. Then write it.

**1**    d
- ime
- ike

**2**    b
- ike
- ite

**3**    p
- ine
- ime

**4**    k
- ite
- ine

**5**    t
- ime
- ite

**6** 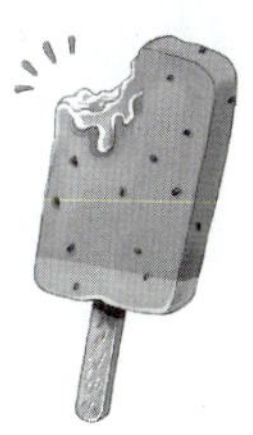   b
- ine
- ite

# Check the correct picture.

**1**  line

**2**  time

**3**  hike

**4**  bite

# Circle the correct word.

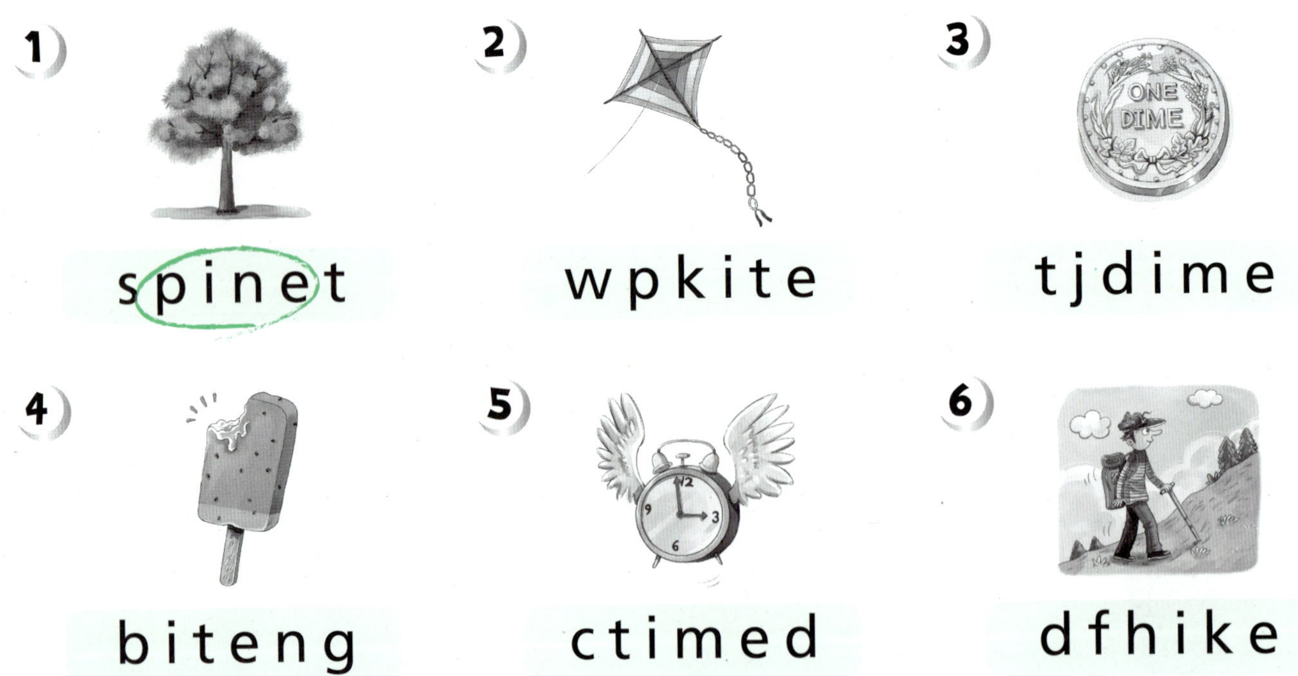

**1)** s p i n e t

**2)** w p k i t e

**3)** t j d i m e

**4)** b i t e n g

**5)** c t i m e d

**6)** d f h i k e

# Look and write the word.

1. b | ike

2. h | ike

3. d | ime

4. t | ime

5. p | ine

6. l | ine

7. k | ite

8. b | ite

# Unit 4 Long Vowel i

Match the picture to the correct ending letters.

1 

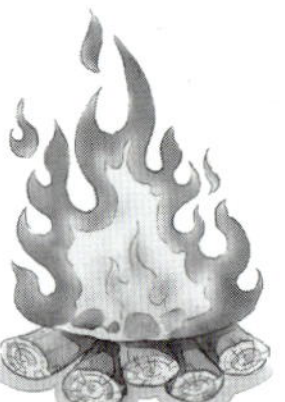

-ide

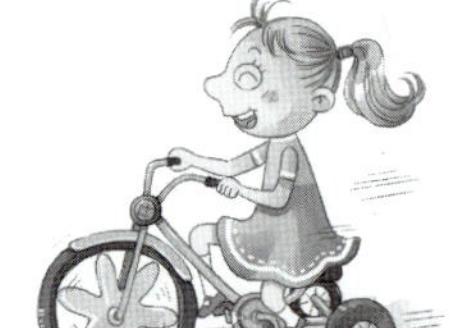

5 

2 

-ire

6 

3 

-ive

7 

4 

-ipe

8 

Trace and write.

-ide ride wide

-ipe pipe wipe

-ire fire tire

-ive five dive

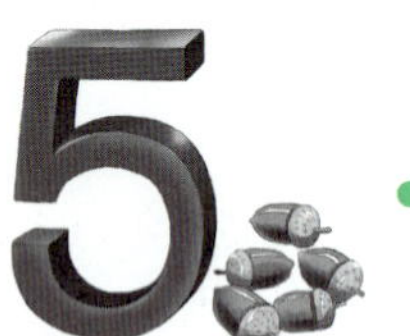

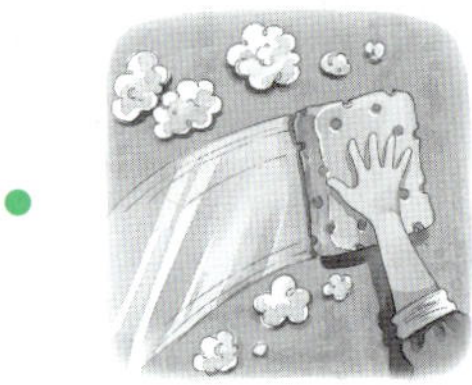

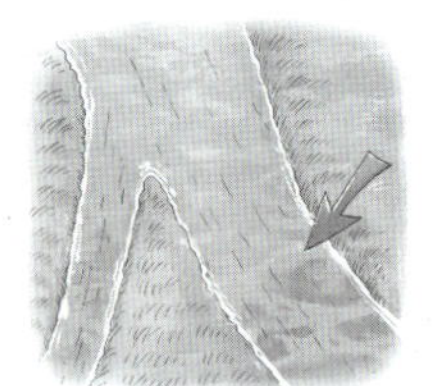

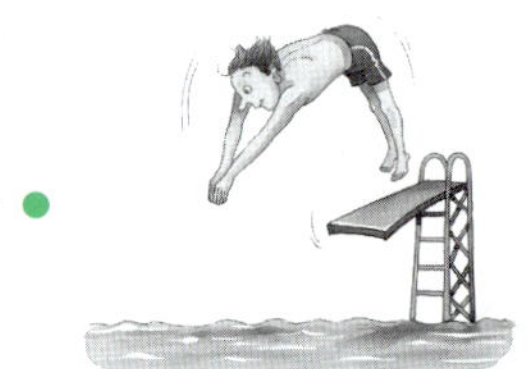

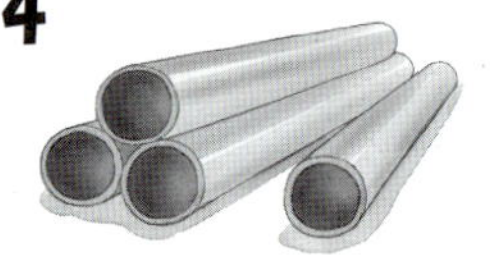

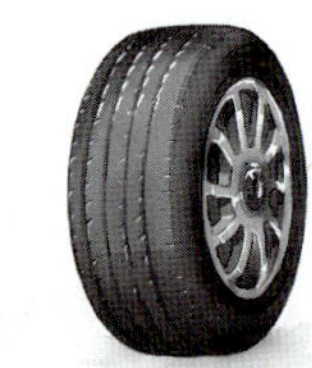

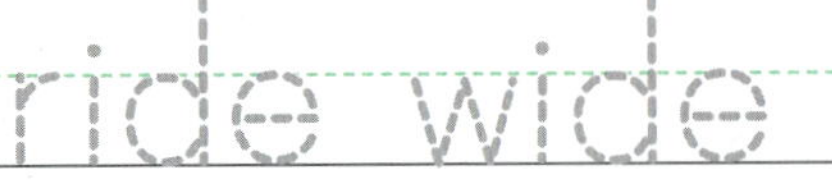

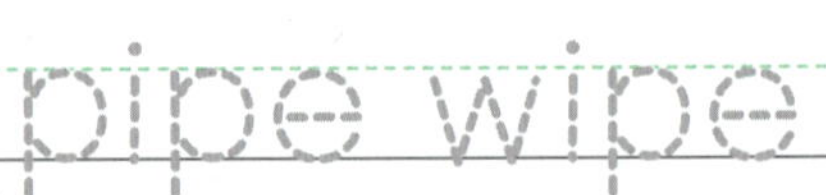

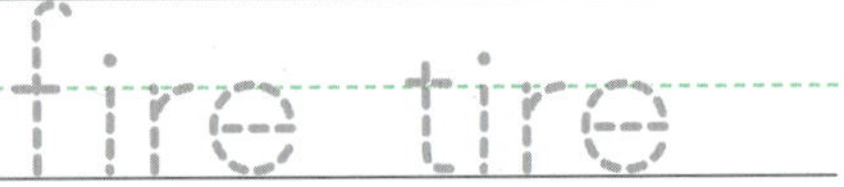

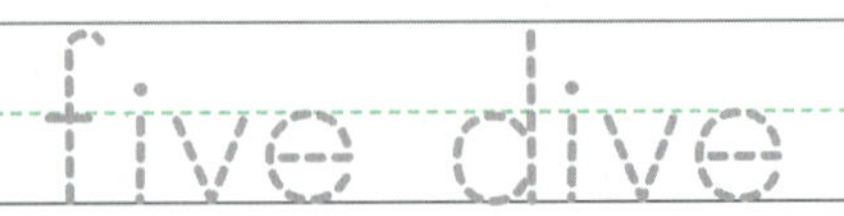

# Match and make the word. Then write it.

**1**   **d** •   • ive  ________
         • ipe  ________

**2** 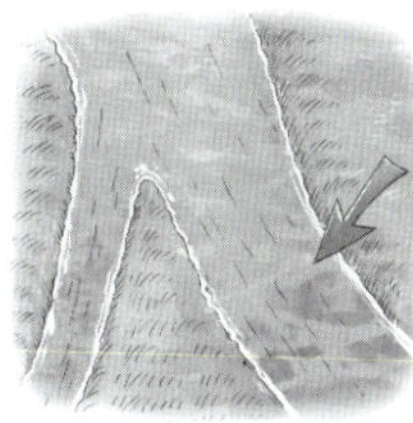  **w** •   • ire  ________
         • ide  ________

**3**   **f** •   • ive  ________
         • ire  ________

**4**   **w** •   • ipe  ________
         • ide  ________

**5**   **f** •   • ire  ________
         • ive  ________

**6**   **t** •   • ire  ________
         • ide  ________

## Check the correct picture.

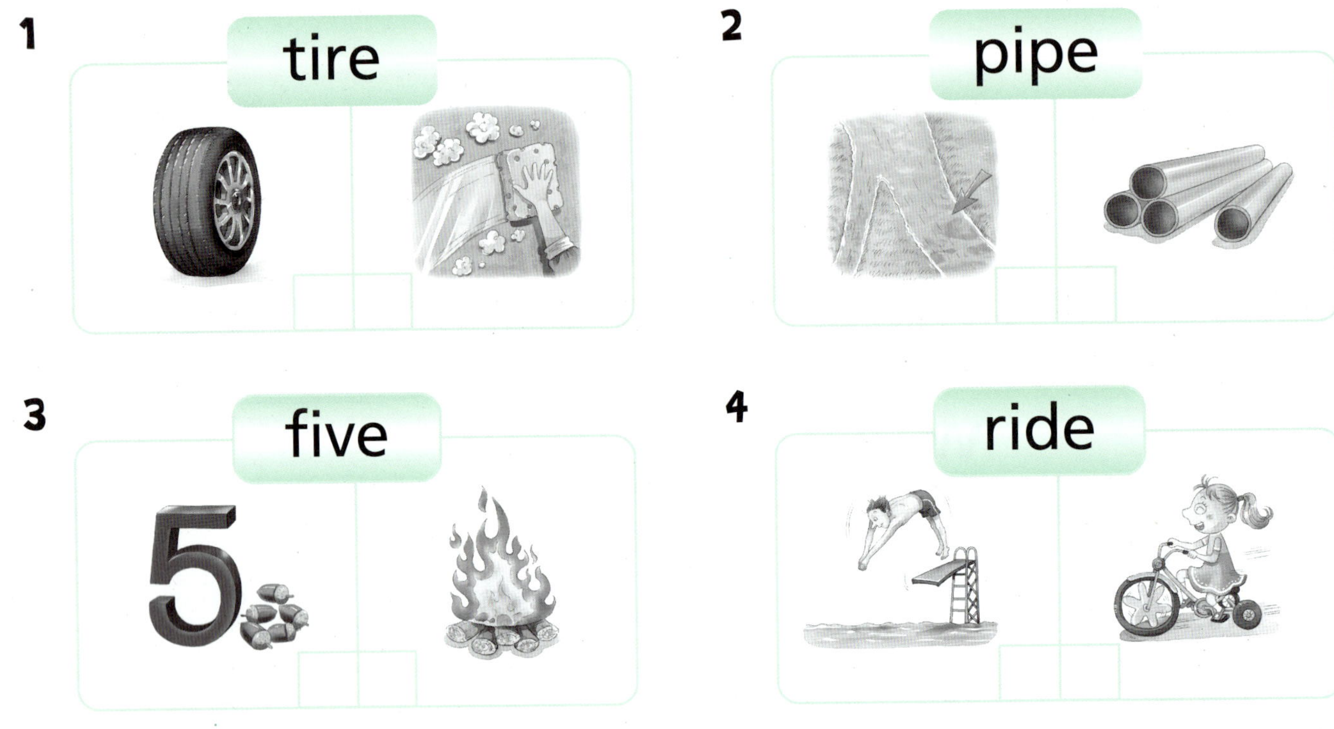



## Circle the correct word.

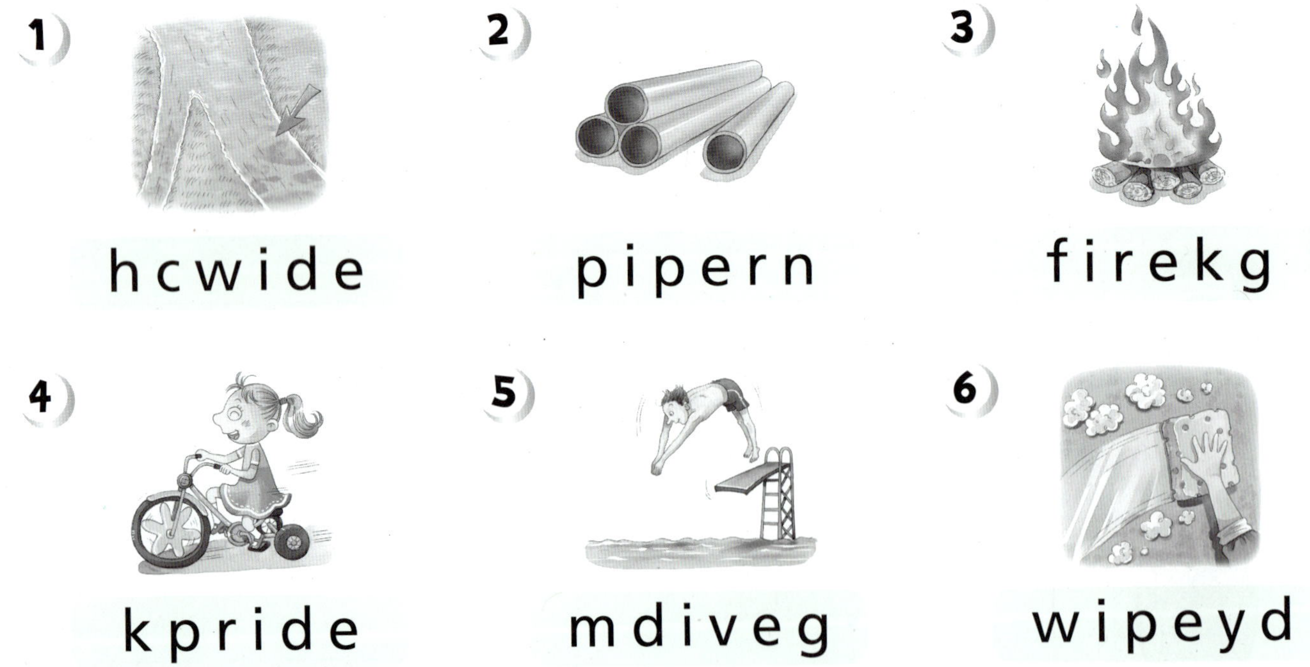

# Look and write the word.

**1** r | ide

**2** w | ide

**3** p | ipe

**4** w | ipe

**5** f | ire

**6** t | ire

**7** f | ive

**8** d | ive

**Look and circle the correct word.**

**1** 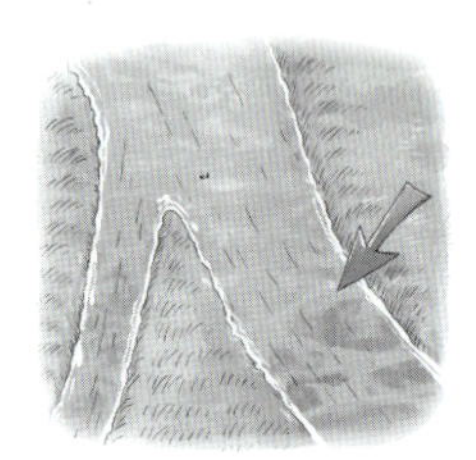

wide
line
wipe

**2** 

tire
ride
bike

**3** 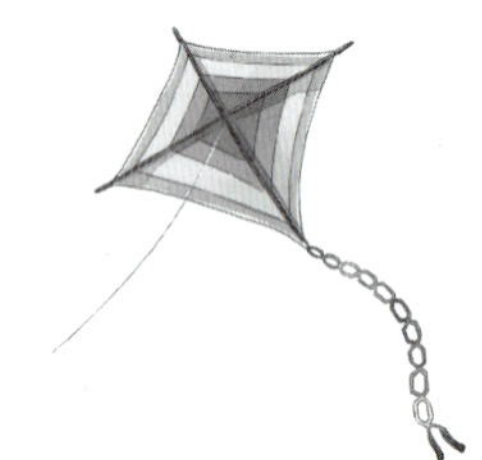

kite
pipe
five

**4** 

pine
fire
bite

**Look and circle the correct picture.**

**1** w**ipe**    

**2** d**ime**   

**3** f**ive**   

## Match and make the word. Then write it.

**1**

t •          • ite
_______________

**2**

h •          • ire
_______________

**3**

r •          • ike
_______________

**4**

p •          • ide
_______________

**5**

b •          • ine
_______________

**6**

d •          • ive
_______________

Circle the correct word and write it.

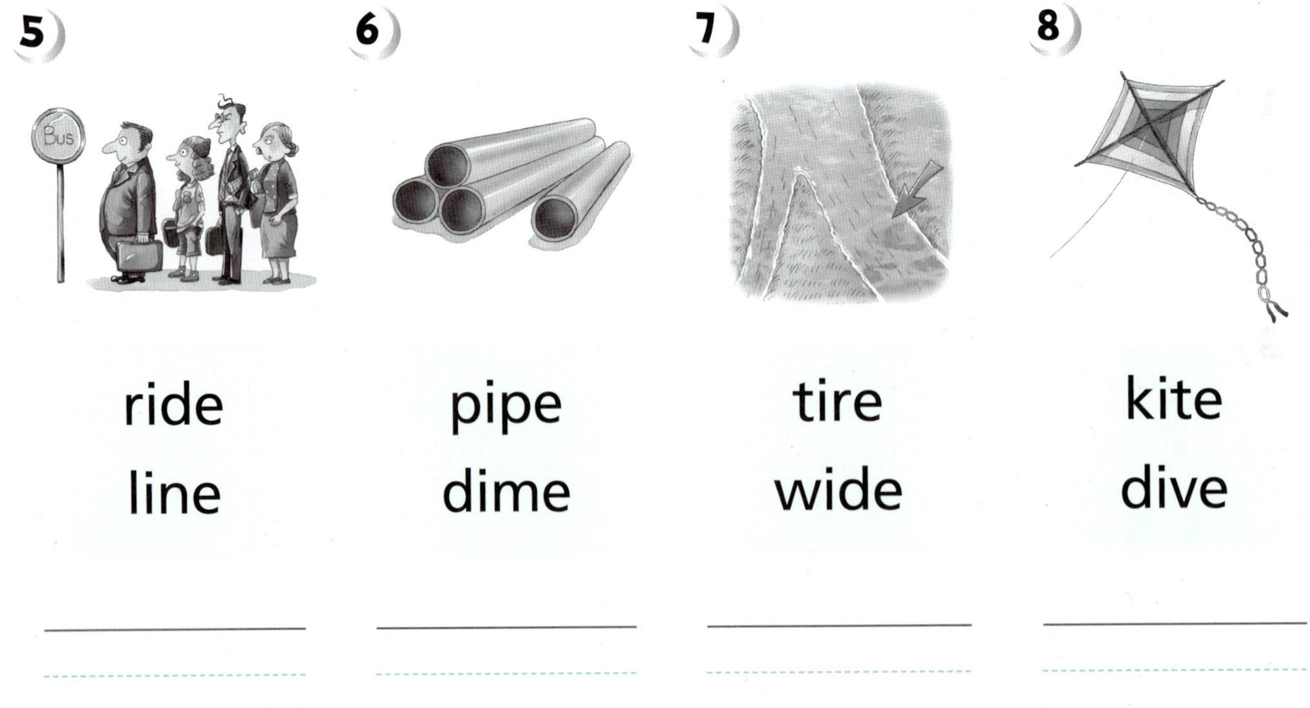


1
bike
bite

2
wipe
fire

3
five
pine

4
hike
time

5
ride
line

6
pipe
dime

7
tire
wide

8
kite
dive

# Circle the picture with the same ending letters.

1   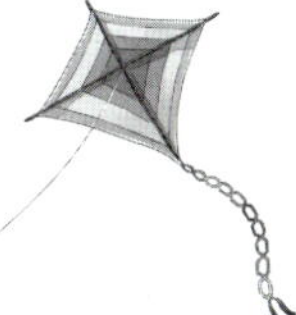 

3   4  

  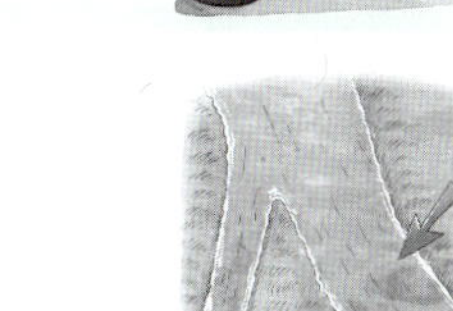 

# Look and write the word.

1  __________

2 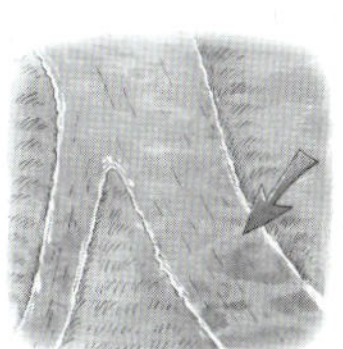 __________

3  __________

4  __________

5  __________

6  __________

# Long Vowel O

Match the given ending letters to the pictures.

1) -ole  2) -ome  3) -obe  4) -one

Trace and write.

-ole  hole  mole       -obe  globe  robe

-ome  dome  home       -one  cone  bone

# Match and make the word. Then write it.

**1**    c    | ole

**2**    b    | one

**3**    h

**4**    d    | ome

**5**    gl    | obe

**6**    r

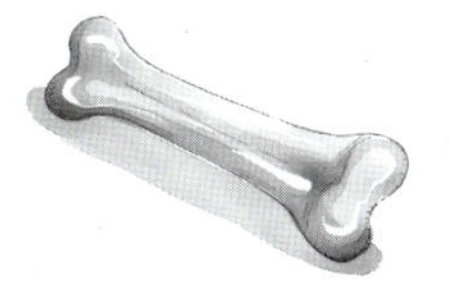

Circle the picture with the same ending letters.

**1**

**2**

**3**

Circle the correct word.

# Look and write the word.

1. h | ole

2. m | ole

3. gl | obe

4. r | obe

5. d | ome

6. h | ome

7. c | one

8. b | one

# Unit 6 Long Vowel O

Look and circle the correct ending letters.

1) 

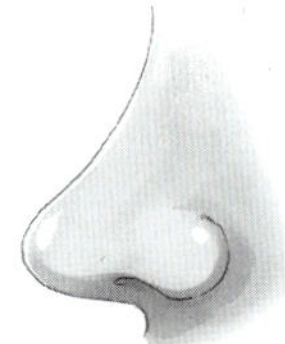

ose ope

2) 


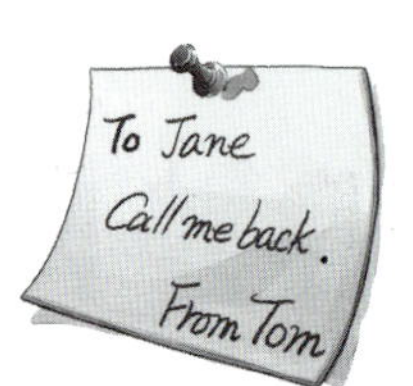

ote ose

3) 

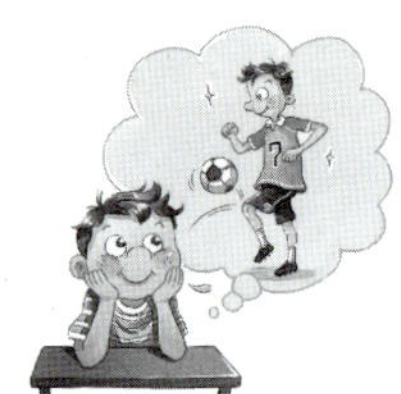

ote ope

4) 

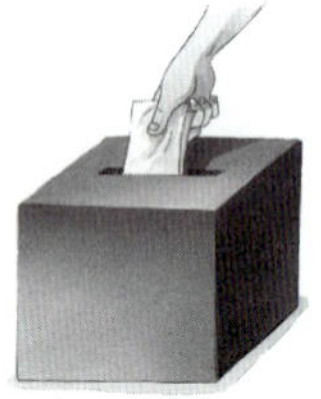

ope ote

5) 

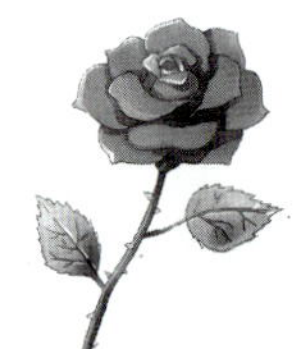

ose ope

6) 

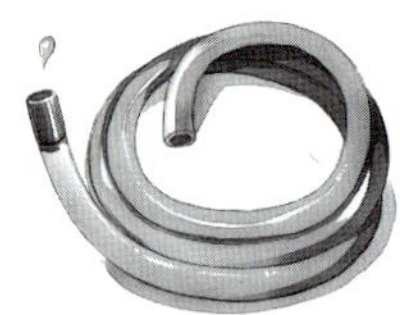

ote ose

Trace and write.

**-ose** hose nose pose rose

**-ope** hope rope

**-ote** note vote

## Match and make the word. Then write it.

1 

**ote**

2

**ose**

3

4

**ope**

5

6

n

p

v

r

h

# Circle the picture with the same ending letters.

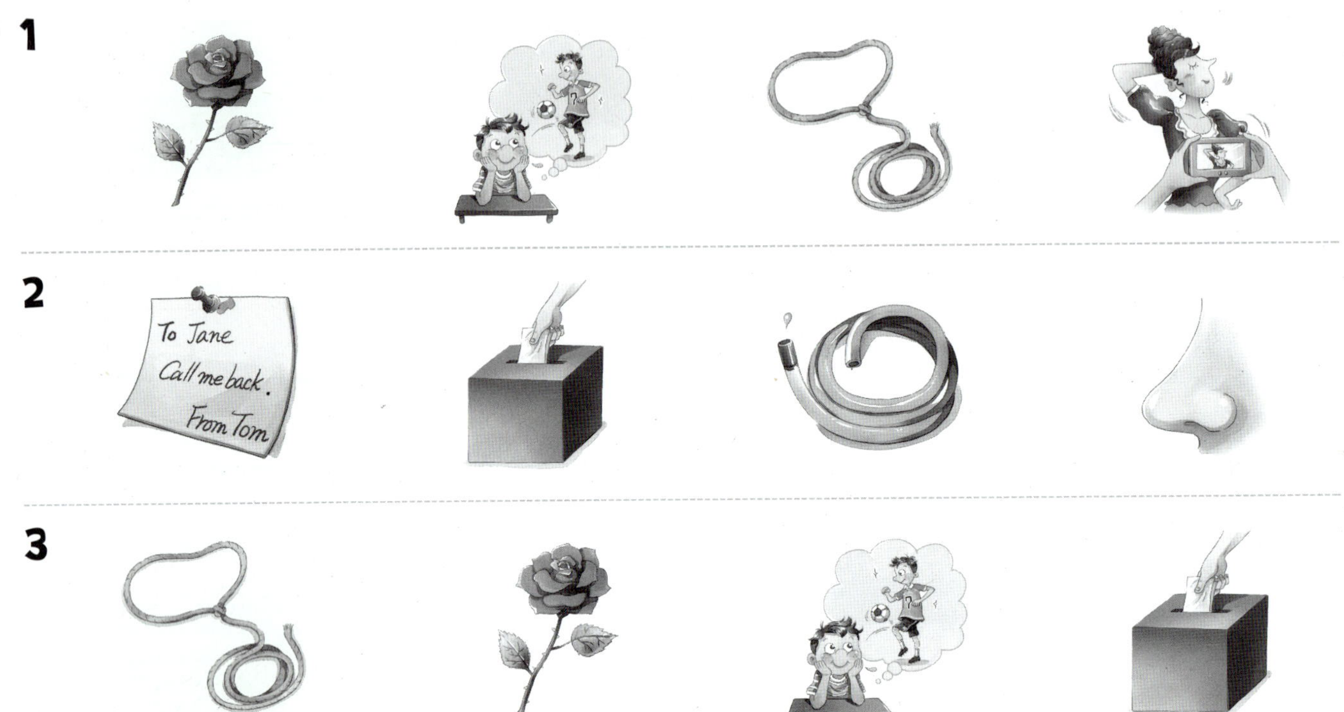

# Circle the correct word.

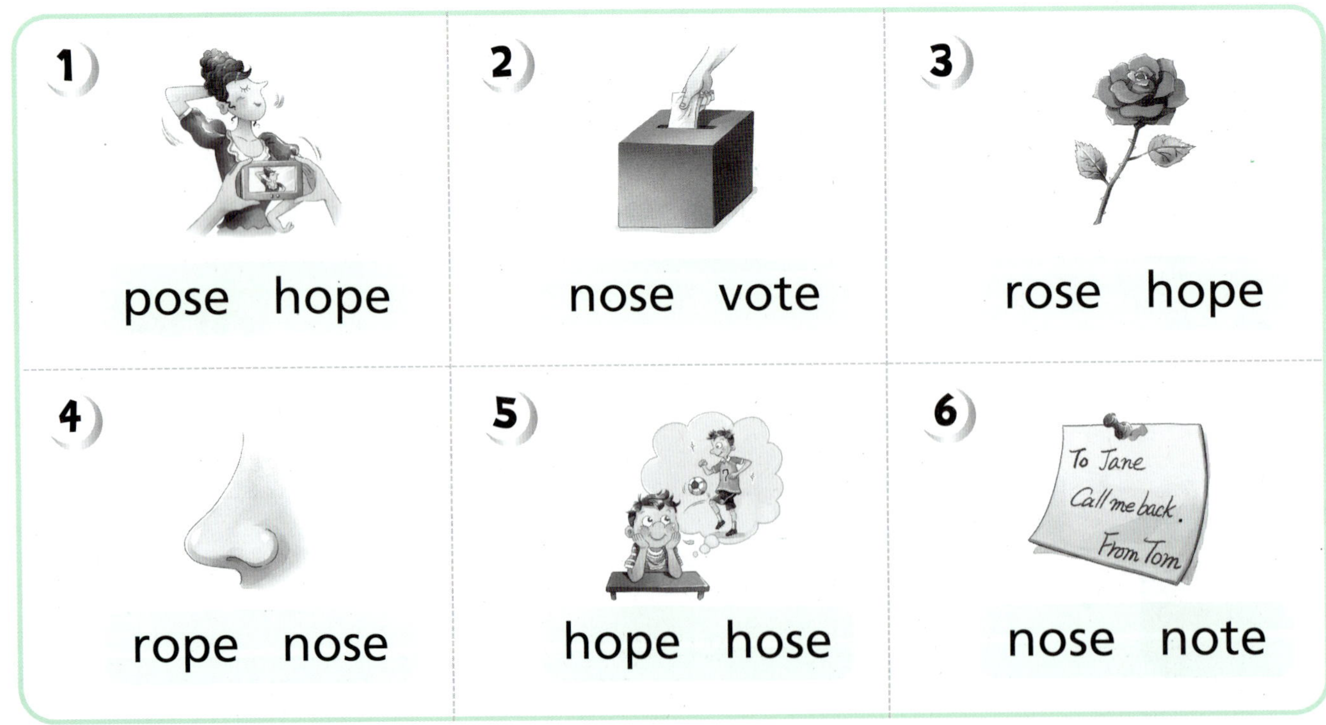

## Look and write the word.

1  h | ose

2  n | ose

3  p | ose

4  r | ose

5  h | ope

6  r | ope

7  n | ote

8  v | ote

# 

Look and circle the correct word.

**1** 
- hole
- dome
- hope

**2** 
- hose
- cone
- rose

**3** 
- bone
- home
- robe

**4** 
- rope
- note
- nose

Look and circle the correct picture.

**1** **h**ose  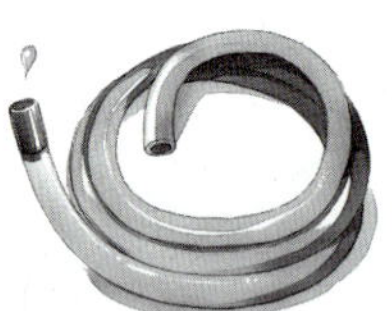 

**2** **b**one 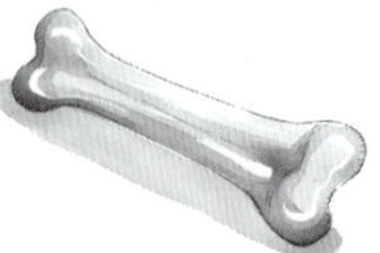 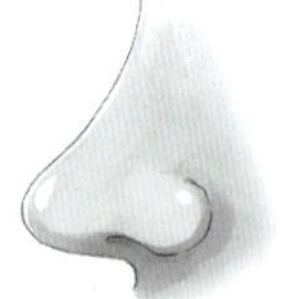 

**3** **g**l**obe**   

# Find and circle the word. Then write it.

s n o s e c b h o p e k f d o m e p z n

**1**

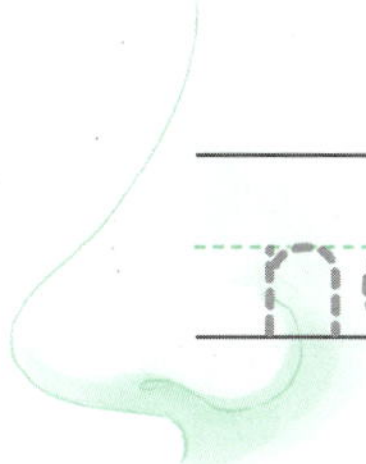

nose

**2**

**3**

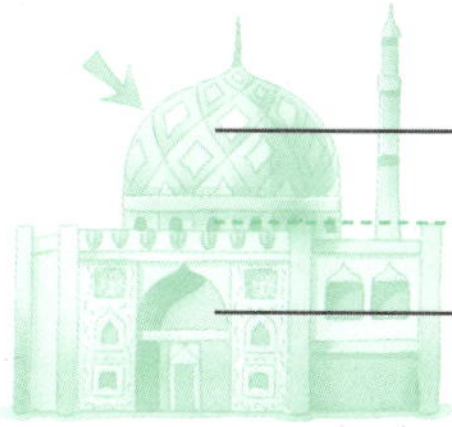

t i r o b e j c f b n o t e c b k p o s e

**4**

**5**

**6**

m o l e s h v o t e v j s d c o n e l g

**7**

**8**

**9**

## Look and write the missing letters.

# Circle the picture with the given ending letters.

**1** **-ose**

  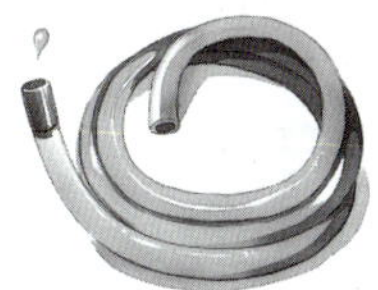

**2** **-ole**

  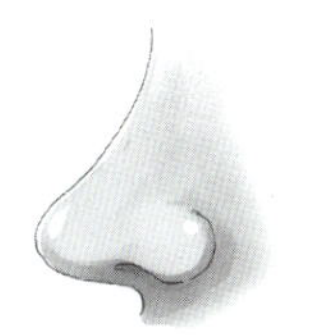

**3** **-one**

**4** **-ope**

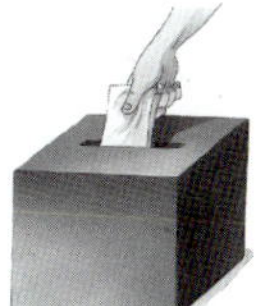  

# Look and write the word.

**1)**   _______________

**2)** 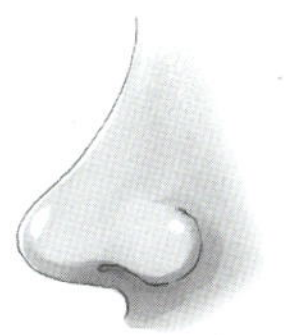  _______________

**3)**   _______________

**4)**   _______________

**5)**   _______________

**6)**   _______________

# Long Vowel  U

Look and circle the correct ending letters.

**1)** 

ube   use

**2)** 

une   ube

**3)** 

use   une

**4)** 

une   use

**5)** 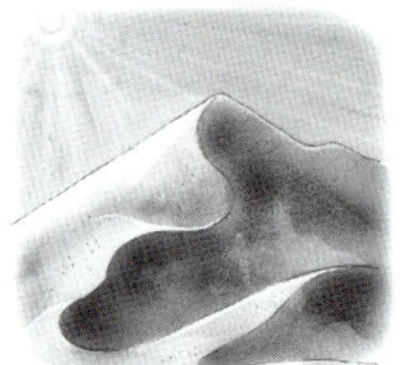

une   use

**6)** 

ube   une

Trace and write.

**-une**   dune   June   tune

**-ube**   tube   cube

**-use**   fuse

# Match and make the word. Then write it.

**1**

c •
- • une
- • ube
- • use

---

**2**

f •
- • une
- • ube
- • use

---

**3**

t •
- • une
- • ube
- • use

---

**4**

J •
- • une
- • ube
- • use

---

**5**

t •
- • une
- • ube
- • use

---

**6**

d •
- • une
- • ube
- • use

Check the correct picture.

**1** dune

**2** cube

**3** fuse

**4** tune

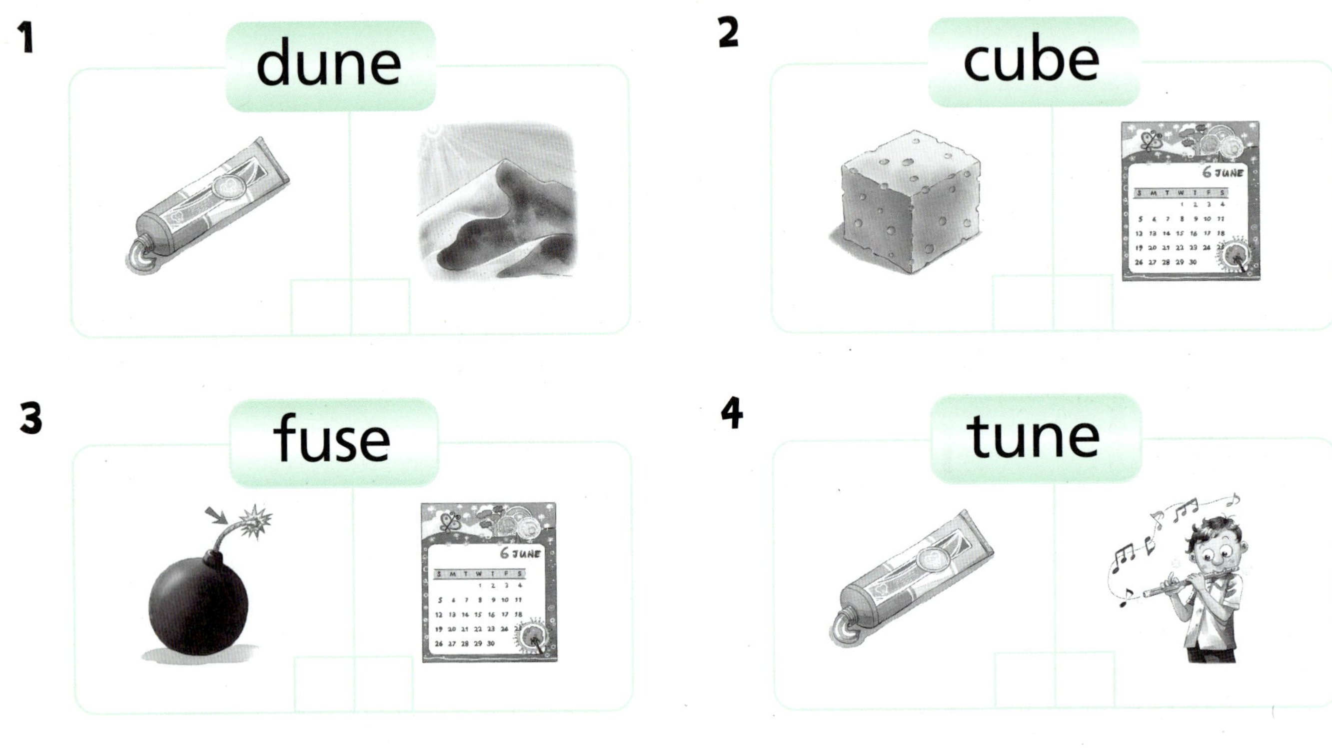

Circle the correct word.

**1)** 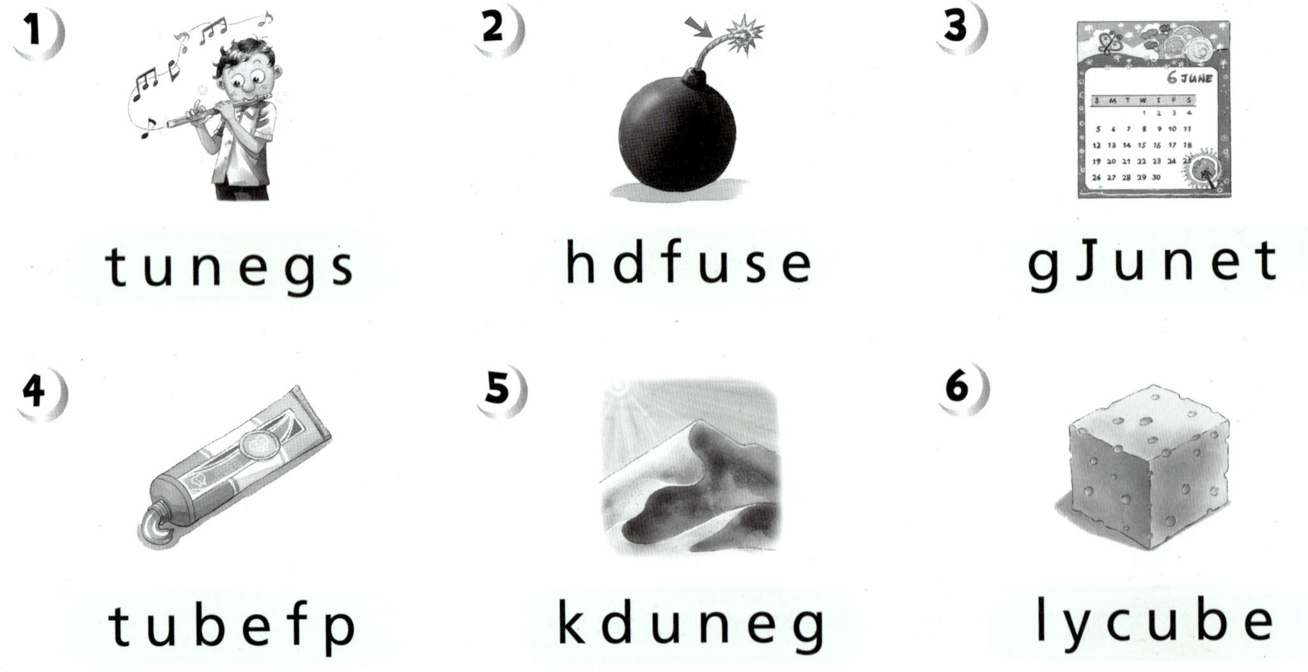

t u n e g s

**2)** h d f u s e

**3)** g J u n e t

**4)** t u b e f p

**5)** k d u n e g

**6)** l y c u b e

# Look and write the word.

**1**    d | une

**2**    J | une

**3**    t | une

**4**    t | ube

**5**    c | ube

**6**    f | use

# Long Vowel U

Match the picture to the correct ending letters.

1

4

2

5

- -ure -
- -ute -
- -uge -

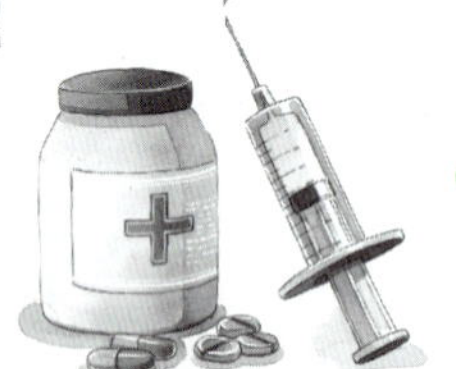

3

6

- -ule -

Trace and write.

**-ure**   cure        pure

**-ute**   cute        mute

**-ule**   mule

**-uge**   huge

# Match and make the word. Then write it.

**1**  m •

- ute
- ule
- uge

____________________

**2**  c •

- ute
- uge
- ure

____________________

**3**  m •

- ule
- ure
- uge

____________________

**4**  c •

- ure
- ute
- ule

____________________

**5**  p •

- ule
- ure
- ute

____________________

**6**  h •

- uge
- ule
- ute

____________________

Check the correct picture.

Circle the correct word.

# Look and write the word.

**1**  c | ure

**2**  p | ure

**3**  c | ute

**4**  m | ute

**5**  m | ule

**6**  h | uge

# 

Look and circle the correct word.

**1** 

dune
pure
huge

**2** 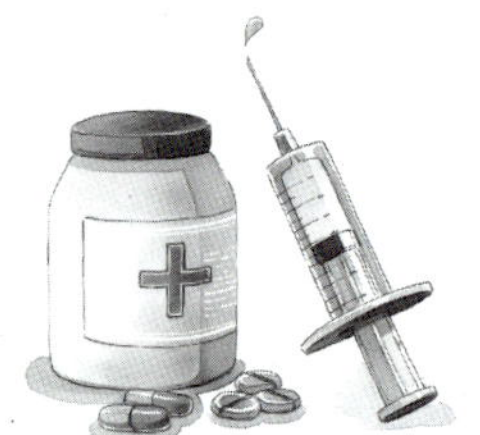

mule
cure
June

**3** 

cube
mute
fuse

**4** 

tube
cute
tune

Look and circle the correct picture.

**1** pure 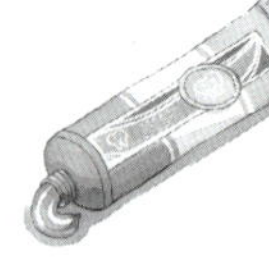  

**2** mule  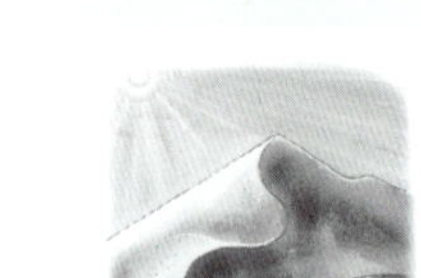 

**3** tune   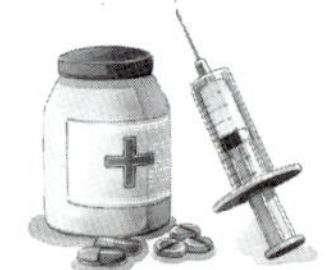

**4** cube   

# Find and circle the word. Then write it.

j c u t e v x w h u g e f n v J u n e k

1

2

3

c u b e d k c u r e g c l n p f u s e z

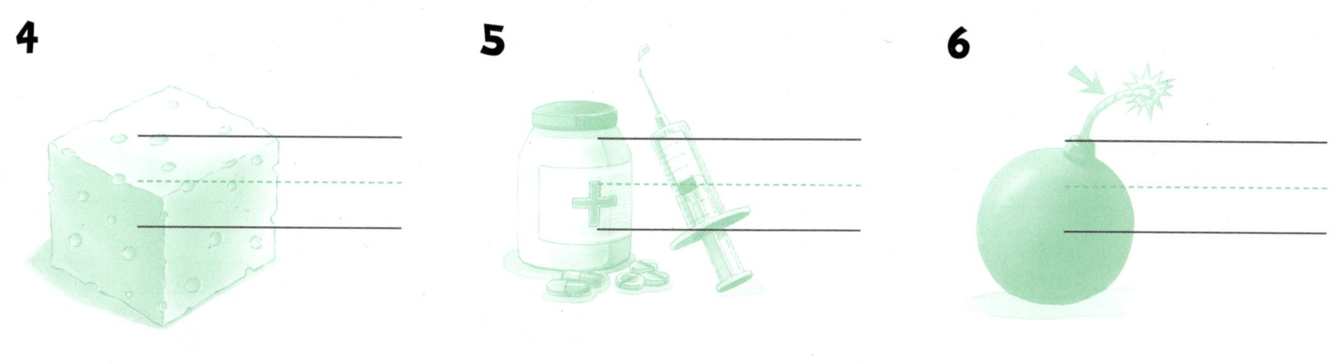

4

5

6

y p m u t e j r s d u n e n t u n e h n

7

8

9

# Look and write the missing letters.

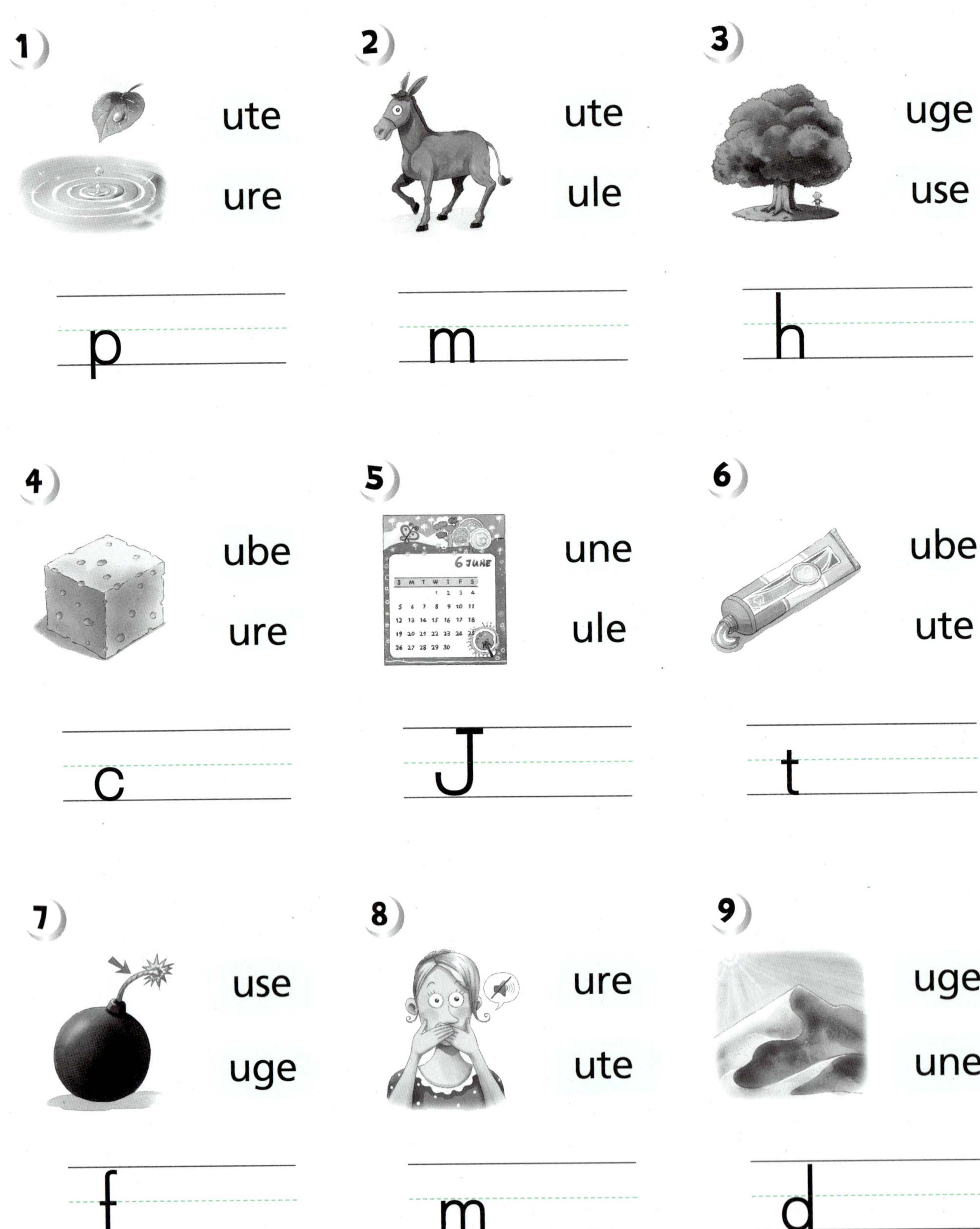

**1)** ute / ure — p______

**2)** ute / ule — m______

**3)** uge / use — h______

**4)** ube / ure — c______

**5)** une / ule — J______

**6)** ube / ute — t______

**7)** use / uge — f______

**8)** ure / ute — m______

**9)** uge / une — d______

## Circle the picture with the given ending letters.

**1**    **-ute**            

**2**    **-une**        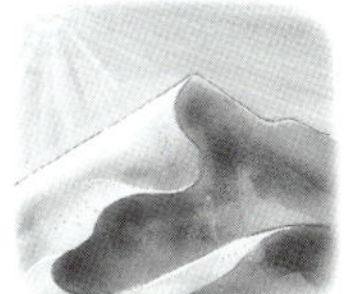    

**3**    **-ure**    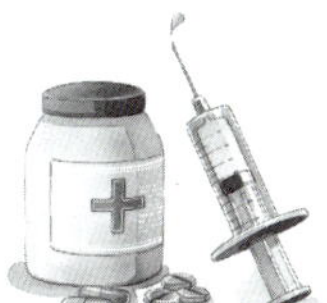        

## Look and write the word.

**1)**  __________

**2)**  __________

**3)**  __________

**4)**  __________

**5)** 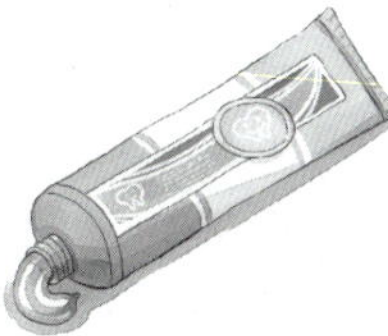 __________

**6)** 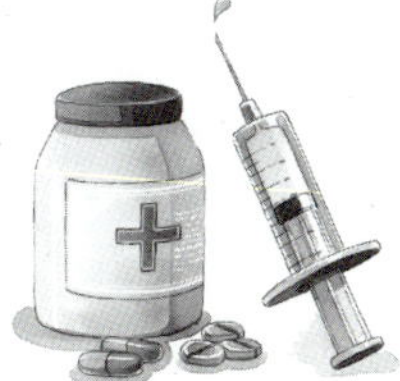 __________

# Phonics wonder